The Thrifty Baker

The Thrifty Baker

Shop, Bake & Eat on a Budget

Hermine Dossou

Photography by
Patricia Niven

WHITE LION
PUBLISHING

For Mum & Steven

Introduction

Ever since I can remember, food is what has brought my family together. We'd always cook a big meal, gather around to eat it, and make memories. We still do.

It's natural, then, that food has become my way of showing love, extending friendship and giving care. I like to put a smile on people's faces, and the more I have honed my skills as a cook and baker, the broader those smiles have become. It's my way of caring, not just for others but for myself too.

Although I made my first cake on my eighth birthday, it wasn't until I became a single mother that my passion for baking blossomed. Money was tight, but I was not going to let that stop me. Baking helped to fill the long afternoons when my son, Steven, was sleeping and it became an important creative outlet.

As a first-time mother, I wanted to feed Steven and myself with nutritious food that was free from preservatives and not too sweet or salty. In order for us to eat well, I had to learn to cook and bake on a budget. And, as caring for my son meant I could only work part-time, it was a budget that didn't stretch very far.

Motherhood quickly made me a thrifty person. I only bought clothes on sale, choosing a couple of sizes above my son's age ready for next season. When I needed a Christmas tree and decorations, I got them on sale for the following year. When I went shopping, I took advantage of club cards and discount vouchers. And I always visited the discount food section of the supermarket to see if there was anything I could work with. I swapped convenience for saving. Ironically, this was the time I experimented most with my cooking and baking.

Life has moved on, but the tips and techniques I picked up in those days have stayed with me. Being an accountant, I look at most things through the twin lenses of costs and savings. I'm pretty good with numbers and this has helped me cost recipes and make savings on my shopping bills. I'm always after quality – but at the most competitive price. I've also learned the importance of planning ahead, forecasting and budgeting in order to achieve the maximum gain from my income.

Above all, I love to be resourceful as a baker and cook, and to make the most of what I have in the fridge or store cupboard. I firmly believe that no solitary carrot, lonely lump of cheese, or half-used carton of cream should ever go to waste if it can be turned into something delicious.

I also believe that we are here to learn from our life experiences, no matter how tough. Although times have been hard for me financially, I am very grateful that this experience has given me the knowledge, skills and motivation to enter *The Great British Bake Off* and build the career in baking that I am so blessed to enjoy. I hope that in some way my experience inspires you too.

About the book

When times are tough and we are on a strict budget, baking might seem like a luxury – an indulgence that's difficult to justify in terms of ingredient costs, energy and, of course, our precious time.

But baking need not be expensive. Swapping convenience foods for homemade is a great way to save money. The tips and techniques in this book will help you become a thrifty baker. I've created a wide range of affordable recipes for all kinds of bakes – recipes that look good, taste gorgeous and are easy to make, yet almost every ingredient has been sourced from the discount store!

I know the importance of having a realistic, concrete benchmark to show just how much can be saved – so I promise I have kept the majority of the recipes under 50 pence (65¢) a portion.

Thrifty people exist at every level of society. They are simply resourceful. A thrifty baker is no different. You can be thrifty in any supermarket you like – it is about being savvy. Read product labels, compare pack sizes and don't pay more when there are cheaper products available of the same quality.

Buying an ingredient is like making an investment; we should aim to get as big a return from it as we can. So managing your ingredients and avoiding waste is just as important as bargain hunting. Whenever I include a pricey-but-worthwhile ingredient in this book, I give suggestions for other bakes it can be used in as well.

I've minimised the use of expensive equipment such as food processors and stand mixers in this book, too. If you don't have exactly the right cooking tools for a recipe, I'll explain how to improvise wherever possible.

None of these recipes take longer than one hour in the oven – many take significantly less – and I've carefully selected baking tins to achieve that. The microwave mug cakes and air fryer recipes are even cheaper on energy.

While saving money lies at the heart of this book, I want to demonstrate that, when it comes to baking, necessity can be the mother of invention. You really can produce exciting and impressive meals, treats and celebratory bakes with limited means.

Equipment

Whilst it can sometimes seem like you need lots of expensive equipment to create impressive bakes, this isn't the case at all. Most recipes can be made with a few basic tools, and if you don't have something, you can often improvise with something else that you already have. Where you do need a specialist item, there are tips that you can follow to ensure that you buy the best quality items for you budget, that will provide good value and last a long time.

Ovens, microwaves and air fryers

Your oven is typically the most expensive piece of cooking equipment you will own, and you may not be able to change it, but it's worth being aware of the differences between gas and electric ovens. It currently costs twice as much to run an electric oven per hour as it does to run one on gas. However, electric fan ovens, which circulate hot air more efficiently, let you cook at a lower temperature or for a shorter time.

Whatever type of oven you have, it's important to make sure that you are using it as efficiently as possible.

When timing is provided in any recipe, realise that this is a guide and also follow your recipe's cues for doneness. Each oven is unique and depending on the type of oven and its age, each will cook differently.

Preheating your oven is important for optimal results in baking. Cakes, pastries, bread and biscuits (cookies) need an immediate injection of heat as they go into the oven. Modern ovens generally only need preheating for 10–15 minutes – don't leave it on while you weigh and mix all your ingredients, or you'll be wasting energy.

Baking in an oven that has not been preheated takes longer than in an oven that has and, with certain recipes, this will affect the end result. The butter will seep out of pastries and destroy the perfect layering and texture. Sponges and bread won't rise properly and will have a disappointing crumb. However, if your recipe asks for toasted nuts, you can do this while preheating your oven, to kill two birds with one stone and save energy. You can also melt butter and toast spices in the preheating oven.

As tempting as it is to keep opening your oven to check your bake, it is best to leave the door closed until the end of the baking time. Every time you open the door, the temperature of your oven drops and more energy is needed to heat it up again. And if you're baking a cake, letting in cold air could cause it to collapse.

If using an electric oven, make the most of residual heat. Switching it off 20 per cent before the allocated baking time and keeping the door closed will enable you to finish the bake with residual heat while saving on electricity. So, if a bake calls for 1 hour baking, switch the oven off after 48 minutes and leave the oven shut till the full time is up. It isn't possible to do this with a gas oven as the residual heat effect is almost non-existent.

Try baking in batches to save energy. If your family likes a particular cake or you make a dessert more than once a week, cook them in batches and refrigerate or freeze them. You can also bake while cooking other things in the oven that require the same temperature – for example, baking a pie or loaf while cooking a casserole or a roast. Be careful not to mix sweet and savoury dishes, however.

Quick microwave and air fryer cakes use much less energy than a conventional oven – no-bake desserts use even less. The average air fryer works at 180°C/350°F, similar to what you might bake a cake at in a conventional oven but requiring less energy. If you have one that needs no preheating, you really hit the ground running.

I've found microwave mug cakes a great way to get my son into baking without worrying too much about the kitchen turning into a bomb site. When cooking them, remember you want the batter only just cooked so that when you place your finger on top, it feels slightly sticky. If it feels completely dry, then you've overcooked your cake.

To be energy efficient when cooking on a hob or stove, it's important to select the right-sized pan for the ring. A small pan on a big ring wastes energy and a big pan on a small ring takes longer to heat, therefore using more energy.

Finally, remember that keeping your oven clean will help avoid energy wastage by ensuring even heat distribution, higher performance and the reduction of hot spots.

Baking tools and tins

Equipment is an important part of baking yet it is tempting to go for the cheapest items. Sometimes it's justified, but on other occasions it's a false economy. It's a matter of knowing when to spend a bit more on good-quality items, and when you can make some savings or improvise.

The smart thing to do is look for good quality, well-made equipment that's available second-hand. It can be even cheaper than 'value' ranges and will perform better and last longer. I bought my first bread maker second-hand eleven years ago – it was someone's unwanted wedding gift. Although I paid half price, I still had to think carefully before buying it. But now it's made so many brioches that it has paid its way and is still going strong.

Internet marketplaces are a useful source of pre-owned (sometimes new) baking tins, as are car boot sales. I recently bought an expensive brand of silicone moulds at a brocante in France. They were so cheap and such superb quality, I just couldn't resist. I do like a bargain!

Scales and measuring
Like most professional bakers, I weigh all my ingredients – including the liquids – in grams. It creates less mess and confusion; you'll use the right amount of each ingredient, save on waste, and ensure the best result.

While this book provides US cup measurements, I really do advise purchasing a scale for reliability and consistency and can't stress the importance enough. You can get one for the price of a cake tin.

Cookie cutters
You can improvise cookie cutters by using glasses, cups and the wide end of your piping nozzles. On the same principle, a large plate makes a great template for cutting a neat tart base. For unique shapes, draw them on cardboard first and cut them out to use as a template, which you then cut round with a knife. It's also worth noting that themed cookie cutters are a fraction of their original price just after Christmas and Easter, so stock up for the following year.

Baking tins/pastry rings/tart tins
I take a long-term view with tins and don't mind paying a bit more for good-quality ones. Aluminium tins last forever, conduct heat well and are excellent value for money in the long run. There are some great Teflon-lined tins out there but they inevitably end up rusted and damaged by sharp objects.

Silicone tins/pans are amazing but need to be cleaned without soap as it can build up in a residue and taint the flavour of your bake. The best way to clean them is to make a paste of bicarbonate of soda (baking soda) and vinegar or lemon juice and rub it on the tins. Let the paste dry, then rinse it away.

If you are a keen baker, it is worth having a couple of cake tins of the same size – they make it easy to do layered cakes and save energy, as you can bake two or three sponges at once.

A large pastry ring is worthwhile if you'll use it regularly – for things like tarts, cheesecakes, layered cakes and pies. It will help you achieve a perfect shape but you can improvise with

Step 1: Cut a 15cm/6in square of baking parchment. Fold it in half from one side, reopen, then fold it in two again from the adjacent side so that you have a cross in the centre.

Step 2: Turn a tall, narrow glass upside down. Place the paper on top, folded side up with the centre of the paper aligned to the centre of the glass. You will have four visible ridges where you previously folded the paper. Using one hand to hold the paper at the top of the glass, pinch a ridge tightly to the glass and fold neatly to one side.

Step 3: Repeat with the remaining three ridges, making sure all the ridges are folded in the same direction.

Step 4: Finally, using both hands, press the four folds tightly to the glass, smoothing the top of the glass with the palm of your hand and stroking the side to secure the creases.

Step 5: Remove the paper from the glass and repeat to make however many cases you need.

Step 6: Line your tin with your paper cases and proceed with your recipe.

the outer rim of a loose-bottomed cake tin.

A good tart tin is a great investment for not only sweet tarts, but quiches and savoury pies. Or you can use a skillet, a small shallow roasting pan or a shallow pie dish of similar size to the one recommended in your recipe.

In this book I've purposely steered away from the loaf tin for a good reason: while they look good, anything baked in a 900g/2lb loaf tin will take at least 1 hour to bake. As a general rule, the same quantity of batter baked in a shallow tin will cook in half the time. You'll need a 23cm/9in round tin, or a 20cm/8in square tin, to cook the same quantity of batter as recommended for a typical 900g/2lb loaf tin.

You can even bake a sponge in a rectangular baking tray (Swiss roll tin/jelly roll pan), then cut and layer it to make a gateau, which saves both time and energy. And making cupcakes rather than a whole cake will cook more quickly and serve more people too.

Cupcake/muffin cases

If you are simply baking for the family at home, silicone cupcake moulds are an economical and environmentally friendly option. You can unmould your cakes onto a plate, decorate them and clean your moulds to be used time and time again.

However, if your cupcakes are to be served outside your home, paper cases will be more hygienic and presentable. They can cost a bit, especially if you are a regular cupcake baker, but you can make your own using baking parchment following my steps (left).

Whisks and mixers

When I was growing up, my mum had a Moulinex Electric hand whisk and we knew better than to touch it behind her back or we would be reminded what time it was! For that reason, many of my first cakes were made using a spatula and a balloon whisk. They still work! But electric hand whisks and stand mixers make the job easier.

If buying new is not an option, try second-hand. Again, with electricals, if I have a choice, I will go for quality because of the warranty cover and the fact that they do tend to last longer. Cheap models break easily because of the poor quality of parts used. I took my time to save up for good machines, and looked out for discount vouchers and store incentives to buy.

Many companies do giveaways as a way to promote themselves on a regular basis – you could find yourself winning free equipment. When buying online, google "free vouchers" together with the shop name before you go through the checkout. You might be surprised at the discount codes you can collect. I still do it to this day.

Baking beans

Ceramic baking beans are pricey so use value brand bags of dried pulses or grains. The cheapest I have found is a kilo of 'essential' rice that was 6.3 per cent the price of ceramic beans from the very same store!

When done with your baking beans, allow them to cool completely then store them away in a jar for next time. If you don't have baking beans, you could line your tart tin with pastry, then line it with baking parchment and place a smaller pastry tin inside to act as a weight.

Rolling pin

A marble rolling pin is heavy, strong and sturdy – which is what you want when you are rolling a cold firm pastry full of butter. And it will last a lifetime. If you need an emergency roller pin (of course rolling pastry is an emergency), you could roll with a glass bottle, as people often did when I was growing up. For safety, be sure to pick a sturdy, strong and smooth bottle – a wine bottle will do the job.

Palette knife

Palette knives make cake decorating a joy. If you don't have one, use a bread knife. The pattern on top of my mocha cake on page 134 was made with a serrated knife. The smooth side of the knife will give your bake a smooth finish.

Cooling rack

These allow air to circulate underneath your cooked cake and cool it quickly. If you don't have one, use your spare oven rack or the grill that comes lodged in your oven tray.

Step 1: Unroll a length of parchment paper and fold the bottom right corner diagonally up to meet the top, forming a triangle. Cut along the side so that you have one large square of paper, then cut the paper diagonally following the crease to create two large triangles.

Step 2: Lay your triangle out in front of you with the point towards you. The tip of your piping bag will be at the centre of the longest side.

Step 3: Fold and slide the opposite ends of the triangle around each other to form a cone shape.

Step 4: Fold the top of the bag down and secure with a fold or with a stapler or sticky tape.

Step 5: Add your icing or chocolate to the bag until it's just over half full. Neatly fold the top end over a few times, so the mixture doesn't flop out.

Step 6: Snip the end of your piping bag, then use it to create writing or patterns on your bakes.

Piping bags

I can talk about piping bags all day but have to admit they are not always necessary. You can often achieve the same result just by scooping the filling onto the cake or slapping the butter cream onto the cake using a spatula, spoon or palette knife.

The type of piping bag you choose comes down to one's budget, the application and the frequency with which you'll be using it, as well as environmental concerns. You can buy sets of reusable bags with a few of your favourite piping nozzles. They will last you a long time and make a good investment. But if you are a regular baker or bake for a living, disposable bags come in handy. Although they are dearer, you can buy biodegradable options.

Alternatively, make your own piping bags using parchment paper. Be warned: they won't hold much filling – I only tend to use them for decorative writing using chocolate and royal icing decorations.

Piping nozzles

Are a great way to get creative. I like to buy them as a set as they tend to be cheaper, but if you're only baking occasionally, you don't really need them. Instead, you can cut the tip off your piping bag in shapes that mimic the shapes of nozzles. For thin straight lines, cut straight across the tip. For thick tubular swirls, cut a slightly rounded curve. For a star shape, cut straight across the tip then cut two small triangles out of the end. For a ribbon effect, cut a tiny sliver from just one side of the tip. For a St Honore nozzle, cut across the tip, then cut a slit in the top about 1.5cm/⅝in deep into the bag.

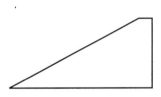

Standard piping bag: Your standard piping bag should look like the above.

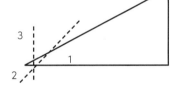

St Honoré tip: Cut a slit in the top about 1.5cm/⅝in deep into the standard piping bag then cut 5mm/¼in across the tip.

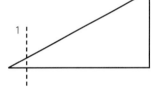

Round tip: Cut the required size hole straight across the tip of your standard piping bag.

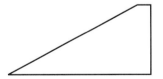

Star tip. Step 1: Start with a standard piping bag.

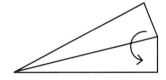

Step 2: Fold the long ends of your piping bag in half so that they meet.

Step 3: Fold the long ends in half again, so that they meet neatly.

Step 4: Make a diagonal cut 3mm to the left(1) and 3mm to the right (2) of the tip.

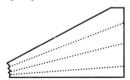

Step 5: Unfold your bag. You are now ready to fill it and pipe a rosette.

Ingredients

Understanding the price of convenience is the key to saving money on your shopping. Anything ready-made or partially processed will cost more, so as often as possible opt for whole ingredients that you can process yourself. Not only are these foods cheaper, there is nothing added to extend their appearance and shelf life.

In general, we thrifty bakers want quality at the most affordable price (or even free). Buying own-brand products from supermarkets is a great way to keep costs down. Own-brand flours, sugars, nuts and raising agents all work in the same way as products from named brands and give just as good results.

Most supermarkets offer reductions on products that are approaching their 'best before' or 'use by' dates. There is an important difference between the two. 'Best before' is about quality – the food is safe to eat after this date but may not have the best flavour or texture; 'use by' indicates that it would be unsafe to eat after that date. Remember dry ingredients like rice, beans and pasta don't really expire; they just lose quality eventually. It's always worth using your common sense when evaluating ingredients, and your physical senses of smell and touch, to judge whether a product is still okay to eat.

When it comes to supermarket deals, it is important to understand the deal you are buying into. Always check the price per 100ml/100g across the range and read the label to make sure you really are getting the cheapest product per unit with the best-quality ingredients. Most supermarkets display price per unit.

As food becomes more expensive, making certain things at home can be a real benefit – butter, yoghurt, jam, sauces and spreads in particular. Plant your own herbs by a window sill and you can add interest to your cooking for next to nothing. If you are lucky enough to have a balcony or garden, why not grow a few things in containers to save money on your fruit and veg bill?

Foraging responsibly is also a great way to bring food costs down. Depending on where you live, you might look for fruit such as blackberries, elderberries, cherries and damsons; herbs like wild garlic and fennel; and edible mushrooms, for which a good identification guide is essential.

Dairy products

Double cream, milk and cheese have a limited shelf life and so are often discounted. With the exception of some cheeses, they can all be frozen for later use. With butter, always look at the ingredient list and the fat content. You will find that the value brand made only from milk with 82% fat content is just as good as premium butter. While you don't often find butter discounted, buying value brands, especially when baking, will save you a few pennies. And buying double cream (whether full price or on discount) and making your own butter from it will save you even more.

At the time of writing this book, a 300ml/10½ oz pot of double (heavy) cream costs around £1 ($1.25). If you make 200g/7oz of butter and 100g/3½oz of buttermilk from it, that's up to £2 ($2.50) cheaper than the price of 200g/7oz of shop-bought butter. The buttermilk can then be used in bread and cakes so there is no waste, and you will have the pride and joy of making your own ingredients. If you make a lot of butter, freeze it in small parcels made from baking parchment.

Powdered milk is another great kitchen staple – economical and long lasting. When I was growing up, my mum used it to make her own yoghurt. I use it to enhance the flavour of some of my custards and enriched doughs. You need 150g/5½oz of powdered milk to make 1 litre/35fl oz of whole milk.

Meat and fish

Buy cheaper cuts of meat for pies and quiches

especially. Chicken thighs and legs taste great and cost less than chicken breasts. If you have time, buying a whole chicken and using it for several recipes works out cheaper than buying chicken pieces. You could, in addition to making a chicken pie, plan to make a stew or curry. The skin and bones from the bird are full of micronutrients so use them for stocks and broths.

The same principle applies to red meat. Instead of diced meat, buy a whole piece and dice it yourself. Braising steak, when cooked correctly, is beautifully tender. Slice it into strips, bulk it up with mushrooms and veg in a cream sauce and you'll have a great pie filling. Minced meat goes a long way too. Instead of several trips to the shop to buy just what you need, buy a bigger size, portion and freeze as soon as you get home. It works out cheaper.

If you have any white fish left over from your bakes, use it to make your own fish cakes or fish fingers. Tinned fish like sardines, tuna and salmon are inexpensive and make tasty and nutritious quiches, pies, breads and empanadas. Remember too that frozen fish (as with vegetables and meat) is generally cheaper than fresh.

Fruits, vegetables, herbs and spices

As a rule, it's cheaper to buy fresh fruit, veg and herbs when they're in season, then freeze them to use at other times of year. Fruits such as berries and mangoes, and veg including onion, pepper and carrots, freeze well for months, retaining their flavour.

Ready-frozen fruit and vegetables are generally cheaper than the fresh variety and are sometimes better in terms of nutritional value, as they are frozen immediately after harvesting. They are sometimes also better for baking, especially when making fruit fillings for cobblers and layered cakes.

Some supermarkets sell wonky fruit and veg at a much lower cost than the 'straight' variety. They come from the same farms, taste exactly the same and would otherwise be thrown away. What's good for our pockets is also good for the planet!

Tinned fruits such as peaches, pineapple, cherries and pears are great for sweet tarts and pies. Their juice can be used to soak a sponge cake, make cocktails, or you can freeze it in ice cube trays and add to iced tea. Nothing need go to waste.

When buying dried herbs and spices, it really pays to shop around. If you have an Asian store nearby, you may find it is much less expensive than your local supermarket and offers a wider range of products. If you buy large bunches of herbs, when they start to wilt, blend them into an aromatic rub that can be spooned into ice cube trays and frozen for use as needed.

Flavourings and essences

Natural flavourings such as citrus zest, herbs and spices are healthier and generally cheaper than artificial ones, and are real friends in the kitchen when you can't afford fancy ingredients.

Vanilla pods can be cost-prohibitive. A quality vanilla extract might be slightly more expensive than artificial essence but a little goes a long way. And with eggy recipes like custards and crème pâtissière, a good vanilla extract can make the difference between a delicious bake and an inedible one.

I often add a dash of alcohol to my cake syrups and creams and always have a cheap bottle at home specifically for baking – it's a great way to add flavour but it is of course optional.

You can enhance the taste of savoury bakes with sugar, honey, stock, Worcestershire sauce or soy sauce. Stock cubes are a staple in West African kitchens and my mum would always add one to her stews. I always use a stock cube in my savoury pie fillings and quiches – they're cheap compared to liquid stock.

Flours

In my view there isn't always a direct correlation between price and quality when it comes to flours. As a thrifty baker, you can get away with using supermarket value brand plain (all-purpose) flour and bread flour – the difference in taste, texture and appearance is marginal unless you are extremely fussy about the end result.

The marked difference between the various brands of flour is in their protein content, so check the packaging and make sure you choose the right type of flour for what you want to bake. For cakes and pastry, you want a flour that has 7–9 per cent protein content; if your recipe calls for plain (all-purpose) flour, you want 10–12 per cent protein content; for bread it needs to be 12–16 per cent protein content; if it needs wholewheat flour, go for 16 per cent protein content.

Gluten-free ingredients

The one time I do tend to splash out on better brands is when I'm making a gluten-free bake and need a good gluten-free flour. Pick a blend that allows you to swap like for like and already has xanthan gum in it. Better to pay a bit more for a blend you know will work than experiment, be disappointed and waste ingredients.

Xanthan gum is a binding agent that does a similar job to gluten in flour – it holds the bake together and stops it crumbling too much. If your flour does not already have xanthan gum, you need to mix some into your flour before adding it to the cake batter. Add ¼ teaspoon xanthan gum for every 120g/4¼oz flour for cakes, ½ teaspoon for every 120g/4¼oz flour for pastry, and 1 teaspoon per 120g/4¼oz flour for bread.

The lack of gluten in gluten-free flour makes it a bit more delicate, so when using it to make pastry, it helps to roll the dough between two sheets of baking parchment. Be aware that some ingredients we may never suspect have gluten may contain it, or might be prepared in an environment where they could have been contaminated with gluten. These include baking powder, icing (confectioners') sugar, custard powder, oats, stock cubes and mustard, so when baking for your gluten intolerant friends, be sure to read the label for traces of unwanted ingredients.

Throughout the book I have added this symbol to indicate when a recipe is naturally gluten-free, such as a meringue, or when simple substitutes can be made to turn it into a gluten-free option. In this case, look to the ingredients list for where you should substitute the ingredient for a gluten-free version. These swaps will all be indicated by the letters (gf) in the ingredients list.

Sugars

Caster (superfine) sugar is caster sugar, whether it's from the value range, discount store or a premium brand. It's true that some are made with cane and others with beet, but you honestly won't notice the difference in a cake. I will always splash out on a little bag of brown sugar, often purchased from the discount store, because it adds deep flavour to bakes. If you can afford the upfront price for a tin of molasses or black treacle, then it pays in the long run to make your own brown sugar. For light brown sugar, you will need 20g/⅔oz of molasses/black treacle and 250g/9oz of caster (superfine) sugar. For dark brown sugar, you will need 40g/1½oz of molasses/black treacle and 250g/9oz of caster sugar. Using your hands, mix the sugar and treacle together until you have a crumble-like consistency.

Honey

Can be sourced cheaply in discount stores and a little goes a long way. I always keep a jar in my store cupboard and, unless I intend to eat it raw, always choose a low-priced one because, once cooked, you don't notice the difference.

Chocolate and cocoa powder

Are must-haves. Two important things to look at on the label are the cocoa and fat content. The higher the cocoa content the richer and more intense the flavour of the chocolate. The fat content of the chocolate will determine what types of bakes it is used for. For example, you will need a higher cocoa content in chocolate brownies to bring out the intensity of the chocolate in your bake. When making chocolate decorations, using a chocolate bar with high cocoa fat content will allow your chocolate to set beautifully. For cookies and chocolate drippings or coatings, don't snub the supermarket value brand chocolate.

It's often possible to pick up discounted chocolate – for example straight after Easter.. These are ideal for baking everything from cookies to cheesecake and chocolate mousse. Easter eggs flavoured with ingredients like coconut, orange, nuts or sea salt can even be incorporated in recipes to liven up the bake.

Cream of tartar, vinegar and lemon

These are important ingredients in making meringue caramel and dough. Vinegar in cooked sugar prevents crystallisation and in meringues, it helps get rid of fat residues that may prevent your egg white from whipping well. In doughs, it affects the gluten development of the flour and therefore helps your dough stay tender.

Fresh eggs

Are cheaper bought in large quantities. They will keep for up to 5 weeks if you have space in your fridge; if not, keep them in a cool place, away from direct sunlight. Don't throw out eggs that have a little blood spot in them – they're still safe to eat and you can scoop out the blood spot with a spoon.

There's no need to bin eggs just because they have passed their best before date. If you are unsure, break them into a cup individually and use your senses. When still fresh, the yolk will hold, and the white will look slimy rather than runny. Smell the egg: a rotten egg has a strong stench and smells of sulphur. You can also pop your egg in a glass full of water. If it sinks to the bottom, it is fresh. If it floats, it is time for the bin. We are trying to be thrifty here, not end up in accident and emergency, so be sensible and, if in doubt, bin the egg.

A good way to save eggs approaching their best before date is to whisk them and then freeze in small containers. Alternatively, separate the eggs, bake with the yolks, and freeze the whites for another day.

Occasionally you will find you need only half an egg for a recipe. Where this happens, mix the remainder with ½ tablespoon of milk to make an egg wash and freeze it in an ice cube tray ready for future baking sessions.

Some recipes ask for custard powder which thickens the mixture and adds colour. If you are not partial to custard powder, use eggs that have a strong yellow egg yolk.

Finally, note that recommendations concerning eggs vary from country to country, especially in the US where they need to be kept refrigerated and have a shorter shelf life, so refer to local advice.

Using up leftovers

Whereas most of the ingredients I use in my recipes are basic pantry staples, such as flour and sugar, some items have a much shorter shelf life. Cooking thriftily means wasting as little as possible! Use the index at the end of the book to find ways to use up your perishable ingredients. Any ingredients that may need to used up quickly – for example, fruit, nuts, chocolate or cream – have been made bold, so you can quickly see what other recipes you can use them in.

If you end up with some leftover pastry, you can wrap it tightly and freeze for up to 3 months, until needed. Try adding finely grated cheese and herbs to your savoury shortcrust pastry scraps: roll thinly and cut out to make biscuits that will work great with cheese or a bowl of soup.

Costing your bakes

Throughout the recipes, I have given an indication as to how thrifty the recipe is:

[1] Less than 50p (65¢) per portion. These recipes use standard pantry ingredients.

[2] Less than 70p (90¢) per portion. These bakes use chocolate or fruit to elevate them.

[3] Up to £1.50 ($1.85) per portion. These dishes are more indulgent and many are designed for special occasions.

It is important to note that whilst some of the savoury bakes are costed with a 3, they will make up a substantial part of a main meal and can still be thought of as thrifty. For example, £1.50 ($1.85) wouldn't normally be considered expensive for a slice of filling homemade steak and kidney bean pie.

Baking techniques

We've all had times when our bakes have gone wrong and there's nothing worse than feeling that you've wasted money when a recipe hasn't come out as you expected. Here I've provided some tips and guidance on some classic baking techniques that are used throughout the book, and that should help you get the most from your bakes.

Tempering chocolate

Tempering gives a shiny finish and snap to your chocolate. I find that it's also more resistant to the heat of your fingers, so it doesn't melt so quickly, leaving marks on the chocolate. The temperature required for tempering chocolate is different depending on whether it's white, milk or dark chocolate (see table, below).

To temper your chocolate, melt two-thirds of it in a heatproof bowl set over a pan of steaming water. Once it reaches the desired melting temperature, bring it down to the desired cooling temperature by adding the remaining one-third of the chocolate. Once it has fully melted, return the bowl to the heat and bring the temperature back up to the desired reheat temperature in the table.

	Melting	Cooling	Reheating
White	40–45°C/104–113°F	26°C/79°F	28–29°C/82–84°F
Milk	40–45°C/104–113°F	27°C/81°F	29–30°C/84–86°F
Dark	45–50°C/113–122°F	28°C/82°F	30–32°C/86–90°F

If you don't have a thermometer, or the time to temper, simply melt your chocolate, use it as intended, then place the finished item in the fridge to set. It is quick and simple, but untempered chocolate is more likely to melt as soon as it is touched and leave marks on your beautiful bake.

Making brown butter

Brown butter is a great way to enhance the flavour of your bake without adding extra flavouring ingredients. Use it for cakes, biscuits, buttercream, sauces and even savoury dishes.

To make it, put the butter in a saucepan over a low-medium heat and allow it to melt and foam. Cook until the colour changes from yellow to nut brown. You will see tiny brown specks forming on the base of the pan and the butter will develop a nutty, toffee-like aroma. As soon as it does, remove the pan from the heat. Strain the butter through a fine-mesh metal sieve, then place in a heat resistant jar at room temperature to cool completely. You can store it in the fridge for up to 2 weeks or freeze it for up to 3 months.

Making genoise

Genoise is my absolute favourite sponge. It doesn't demand a lot of ingredients and it can be cooked in just 15 minutes.

I like my genoise to be light-as-a-cloud

and the knife to cut through it like butter. For that reason, I substitute a third of the plain (all-purpose) flour required with cornflour (cornstarch).

Traditional genoise does not contain baking powder, but if you are new to the genoise game, you might want to include some: a little baking powder provides a safety net, so that your sponge can still rise even if you've lost most of the air when folding in the flour.

To ensure success, it's also important that everything is prepared before you start whipping your eggs and sugar. You don't want the egg mixture sitting around deflating while you're preparing other things.

If preferred, you can choose to whip the egg and sugar over a bain-marie. The heat from the bain-marie helps stabilise the air bubbles and therefore will prevent your batter deflating.

Working with pastry

Unlike bread, you want your pastry dough to be short, so it is often best to use soft flour, which has less protein than strong bread flour. Some pastry recipes may call for bread flour, so it's important to avoid overmixing your dough, so stop as soon as it comes together.

Most pastry doughs are full of butter, so you want to work with cold dough and avoid over-handling it. Keep your dough refrigerated as much as you can and where possible, divide it into batches and only work with one batch at a time.

I am a great believer in making large batches of pastry and keeping them portioned in the freezer so that they're ready to bake. Weigh the dough in the quantity you're likely to use it, then wrap it in an airtight bag and freeze for up to 3 months.

Working with biscuit dough

It might seem counter-intuitive when I've been talking so much about saving energy, but with biscuits, it's often better to bake one batch at a time as you'll get a far better result. They will be golden underneath and on the surface.

When you put one tray on the bottom shelf of the oven and another on the top, the heat does not circulate as efficiently. Doubling up trays means you end up with the biscuits on the bottom tray having a crisp bottom and a beige top and the top-tray biscuits having a golden-brown top and a soft bottom! Given most biscuits cook in 8–12 minutes, they use comparatively little energy.

The only time I cook two shelves of biscuits at once is when the colour of the biscuit is irrelevant because it is going to be covered in icing or chocolate.

Having said that, making large batches of dough and freezing it is a great way to have biscuits and cookies on tap. Scoop the mixture onto a tray lined with baking parchment as if you were about to bake them. Quick freeze, then transfer them to a freezer bag and freeze for up to 3 months.

Whipping cream

You will invariably hear terms like 'soft peak' and 'stiff peak' when it comes to whipping cream. As a cake maker, the important thing to know is that fresh cream continues to whip even when you stop whipping and start handling it with a spatula or piping bag!

Cream that has been whipped too far begins to split and starts turning into butter. This is why all my recipes call for 'soft peaks'; it's advisable to whip your cream just until it forms soft peaks then allow it to reach stiff peak as you begin to pipe it or spread it onto your cake.

If you do overwhip your cream, you can fix it by adding a little extra cold liquid double (heavy) cream and mixing slowly. Keep adding and mixing gently until the cream looks smooth again. Depending on how far you overwhipped it, you may need as much as one-third of the original quantity to correct it. You may also need to adjust the sugar.

If you have whipped it beyond repair, all is not lost! Continue whipping until it turns to butter. Don't worry about the butter being sweet – you can use it to bake sweet treats.

Making European buttercreams

When making European buttercreams, ensure the butter is at a similar temperature to the meringue or custard you're adding it to. If not you will end up with a split buttercream in the case of French or German buttercreams, and with a pool of butter in the case of Swiss or Italian meringue buttercreams.

To fix a French or German buttercream that has split, you want to place your bowl of buttercream in warm water and keep whipping until it is smooth. To fix a runny Italian meringue or Swiss meringue buttercream, put it in the fridge for 15 minutes (depending on how cold your fridge is), then whip the mixture and return it to the fridge for another 15 minutes; repeat until you have a consistent, thick buttercream.

Making caramel

Making your own caramel is far cheaper than buying ready-made. It can be stored in the fridge for up to 1 month or frozen in an airtight container for up to 3 months.

When making caramel, one of the main concerns is sugar crystallisation. This is where you end up with lumps before the caramel has had the opportunity to cook. To prevent this, you want to start your caramel with wet sugar that has started to dissolve. The easiest way to achieve that is to add the sugar to the water – not the other way round. Wait a few minutes for the water to completely soak the sugar before starting the cooking process. Next, adding something acid (a couple of drops of lemon, vinegar, or a pinch of cream of tartar) will prevent crystallisation.

You want to start cooking your sugar syrup over a medium–high heat until it begins to change colour. As soon as you notice some colour, reduce the heat and be patient while your caramel reaches the right colour. The lower heat will allow you to better control the colour, as caramel can burn fast.

Finally, you can add butter, salt and double (heavy) cream to your caramel to create different sauces. Bottled caramel sauces are a great gift idea come the festive season. Put them in clean recycled jars and decorate with labels, ribbons and paper, all recycled too.

Bread and yeasted doughs

For a successful bread, you want good formation of gluten strands and slow fermentation to develop an intense flavour. With yeasted dough, the type of flour you use, and its protein content, will determine how elastic the dough is. High protein flour produces tough dough and chewy bread which is desirable in a white loaf.

I prefer to leave my yeasted doughs to slowly ferment overnight, to intensify their flavour. Ideally you want to start the fermentation process at room temperature and then slow it down overnight in the fridge. If that's not an option, leave the dough in a warm place and it will typically double in size in about an hour. If in a hurry, you can help the dough prove quickly by placing the covered bowl on the shelf of your oven (with the heat off) and sitting a bowl of steaming hot water on the floor of the oven – it should double in size in around 30 minutes.

Bread

Design your own focaccia

 20 minutes + proving   30 minutes | 1 loaf   1

425g/15oz/1¾ cups plus 2 tbsp
   lukewarm water
10g/⅓oz/2 tsp fast action dried
   yeast
80g/2¾oz/⅓ cup olive oil
500g/1lb 2oz/3⅔ cups strong
   white bread flour
10g/⅓oz/2 tsp salt
1 tbsp butter

For the toppings
1 head roasted garlic (optional –
   see pages 28–9)
2 tsp chopped fresh rosemary,
   chives, oregano or parsley
   (optional)
2 tbsp grated Parmesan or other
   cheese (optional)
1 tsp sea salt flakes

Focaccia is a simple bread that allows you, a bit like a pizza, to put anything you want on top. It makes a great alternative to the usual white tin loaf. Here, I give you the recipe for the dough and you choose the topping! I have a few suggestions, but really, I want to encourage you to make this recipe your own. You could try adding vegetables, such as chopped peppers or red onion, soft or hard cheese, preserves, tinned fish or even cured meat.

This recipe has a high water content, which creates a lot of air bubbles, so don't worry about your dough looking sticky. It's one of those recipes that truly benefits from overnight fridge fermentation but also has the flexibility to be baked on the same day. But slow fermentation will develop the flavour and give a beautiful crust, so do consider planning ahead.

- -

In a large bowl (or in a stand mixer fitted with a dough hook attachment), combine the warm water and yeast and mix well. Add half of the olive oil, plus the flour and salt and mix until the flour is all incorporated and you have a sticky dough.

Drizzle over half the remaining olive oil, then cover with some cling film (plastic wrap) or a damp tea towel and place in the fridge overnight, or for up to 48 hours. If you want to bake it on the same day, place your dough in a warm place to prove for about 2 hours, or until it has doubled in size.

When ready to proceed, use the butter to generously grease a rectangular 23 x 33cm/9 x 13in baking tray, roasting tin, glass dish, skillet or any ovenproof dish of similar size. Punch down the dough, then tip it into the dish. Oil your fingers and press them deeply into the dough to stretch it to fit the dish. Leave it to rise again: if the dough is already at room temperature, an hour will be sufficient; if it was kept in the fridge overnight, allow up to 3 hours as the dough will need to get to room temperature again before fully proving.

Preheat the oven to 220°C/200°C fan/425°F/Gas 7. Grease your fingers with the remaining olive oil and press them deeply into the dough to make dimples all over the top of the loaf.

Now for the toppings. If you're using roast garlic, mash the cloves and spread them over the top of your focaccia, and/or sprinkle over the herbs and cheese. To finish, sprinkle the dough with any remaining olive oil and the sea salt flakes. Bake for 30 minutes, or until risen and golden.

Depending on the toppings used, the bread will keep in an airtight container for up to 3 days, or it can be frozen for up to 3 months.

Country bread (pain de campagne)

 35 minutes + overnight fermenting   40 minutes | 2 loaves   1

For the starter (night before)

400g/14oz/3 cups strong white
    bread flour
5g/⅛oz/1 tsp fast action dried
    yeast
5g/⅛oz/1 tsp salt
260g/9oz/1 cup plus 1 tbsp water

For the dough

300g/10½oz/2¼ cups strong
    white bread flour, plus extra
    for dusting
100g/3½oz/¾ cup rye flour,
    or spelt, wholemeal, or plain
    (all-purpose) flour
5g/⅛oz/1 tsp fast action dried
    yeast
10g/⅓oz/2 tsp salt
280g/10oz/1¼ cups water

For garnish

rolled oats or seeds such as
    sunflower, flax, sesame, poppy

There is nothing quite like treating your household to the smell of freshly baked bread in the morning and, for the baker, nothing like the look and crackling sound of bread that has been freshly made. This recipe makes two loaves so you can freeze one for later in the week. Have it as toast with almost anything, use it for sandwiches, serve with soups and turn the last few slices into croutons.

I think of this recipe as a cross between a quick bread and a sourdough. It uses a pre-ferment, but you don't have to wait as long as you would with a sourdough starter. All you need are four simple ingredients – some flour, yeast, salt and water – and no special kitchen equipment. It does take some planning ahead, as the starter needs to be prepared the evening before, but as with most yeasted dough, the secret to its irresistible taste is this slow fermentation.

Adding some oats to the top of the loaf not only looks pretty but tastes great too. I encourage you to bake with what you already have in the pantry, so feel free to substitute with seeds. You can also use this recipe as a base for flavoured breads and fold some roasted garlic, herbs, cheese, nuts or chocolate into your dough towards the end of the kneading process, before shaping your bread.

The night before you wish to bake the bread, make the starter. Put all the ingredients in a bowl, taking care to avoid direct contact between the salt and the yeast as this can hinder the yeast's growth. Mix until well incorporated and leave the dough at room temperature for 1 hour to start the fermentation process, then refrigerate overnight.

The next day, put all the dough ingredients in a large bowl. Add the starter and mix to combine. Tip the dough onto a lightly floured surface and knead for about 10 minutes. If you choose to use a stand mixer, put all the ingredients in the bowl and, using the dough hook attachment, mix on low speed until incorporated, followed by 5 minutes or so on medium speed.

If you want to add extra ingredients such as roast onion or garlic, seeds, or chocolate chips, now is the time to fold them into your dough.

Shape the dough into a ball, cover it with a tea towel and set aside for 1 hour.

Divide the dough into two equal pieces and shape them into rounds (boules). Generously flour two tea towels and get two bowls ready.

Roll the top of each boule in the oats or seeds and place one on each tea towel. Sit them in the bowls, cover and allow to prove in a warm place for 1 hour 20 minutes, or until doubled in size. If your kitchen is cold, putting them in the oven (with the power off) and adding a small bowl of boiling water at the base of the oven is a good way to encourage the dough to rise.

About 20 minutes before your loaves have fully risen, preheat the oven to 260°C/240°C fan/475°F/Gas 9 (removing the bowls from the oven if necessary).

Gently tip your loaves each onto their own sheet of baking parchment. Using a razor blade or a sharp knife, score the bread. I love baking my bread in a large cast iron pot – it traps the moisture and gives the bread a beautiful crust. Use the edges of the baking parchment to transfer one of your loaves into the pot, if you have one, and pop the lid on. If you don't have a pot, simply transfer the loaf, on its parchment, to a heavy baking tray. Put the second loaf in the fridge while the first one cooks to slow the fermentation process.

Put your bread in the oven and, if you are not using a pot with a lid, carefully place a bowl of boiling water at the base. Close the door quickly to catch the steam generated; the steam is what gives your bread that beautiful crust. Bake for 40 minutes or until the bread is golden brown and sounds hollow when tapped on the bottom. Once the first loaf has baked, transfer the second one from the fridge into the pot or onto the tray and bake.

Although it's very tempting to eat straight away, allow your bread to cool completely before slicing. The baked loaves can be frozen for later during the week, or for up to 6 months.

Rustic no-knead rosemary and roasted garlic bread

 20 minutes + resting and cooking the garlic 40 minutes  1 loaf 1

380g/13½oz/1½ cups plus 2 tbsp lukewarm water

7g/¼oz/1½ tsp fast action dried yeast

450g/14oz/3¼ cups strong white bread flour, plus extra for dusting

7g/¼oz/1½ tsp salt

7g/¼oz/1½ tsp sugar

1½ tsp finely chopped rosemary

For the roast garlic
1 large head of garlic
1 tbsp olive oil
pinch of salt

If you are a garlic bread lover, like me, this recipe is for you. What's more, you do not need a stand mixer or fancy equipment to make it. And if you don't like garlic? This may well convert you. Roast garlic doesn't have the strong potent flavour of raw garlic – it has a sweet, mild flavour.

Now if, despite this, you remain unconvinced, you can still make this bread. Keep it plain or substitute the garlic with caramelised onion, herbs, dried chilli, olives, sundried tomatoes, even blueberries and lemon – the choice really is yours.

Planning ahead is an important element of being thrifty, so roast your garlic when you are baking other savoury dishes in the oven. Even better is to make a batch of roast garlic that will last you a long time – I've given the method for batch cooking in my tip (opposite). Batch roasting not only saves you time and energy, it means you have ready-roasted garlic and garlic oil on tap to drizzle over bread, pasta and pizza.

- -

Ideally, you want to roast the garlic while you have something else in the oven and it's set to 180°C/fan 160°C/350°F/Gas 4 (or preheat it to that temperature). Cut the garlic bulb in half horizontally and put it on a sheet of kitchen foil. Drizzle with the oil and sprinkle with salt, then fold up the foil to make a parcel. Roast for 40 minutes, or until the cloves are tender enough to mash easily. Squeeze the cloves from their skins and mash them thoroughly with the oil in the foil, then set aside.

To make the dough, put the water and yeast in a large bowl and stir to combine. Add the flour, salt, sugar, rosemary and mashed roast garlic. Mix with a spatula until the flour is fully incorporated and you have a dough (don't worry if it seems quite wet). Cover the bowl with a kitchen towel and set aside in a warm place for 1½–2 hours, or until the dough has doubled in size.

Generously flour a work surface and tip the dough onto it. Using floured hands to prevent sticking, fold the dough onto itself by stretching it from the edges to the middle, creating a round boule.

+ tip

To batch roast garlic:
If you're making a batch of roast garlic, peel the cloves of **4 garlic bulbs**. Put them in a small roasting pan, pour in **100g/3½oz/scant ½ cup olive oil** so that it covers the garlic and sprinkle with **½ teaspoon salt**. Cover the roasting pan with foil and follow the times and temperatures in the recipe. Once the cloves are tender, transfer the garlic and all the oil from the tin to a jar and store in the fridge.

Dredge a clean kitchen towel with flour, sit your boule – seam up – on the towel and place in a bowl. Cover and leave to rest for 45 minutes to 1 hour, or until doubled in size. If you like a thick, hard crust on your bread, prove your dough in the fridge overnight, or for at least 8 hours. The fridge will slow the fermentation and help develop the flavour and crust of your bread.

About 20 minutes before your loaves have fully risen, preheat the oven to 240°C/220°C fan/475°F/Gas 8.

Gently tip your loaf onto some baking parchment. Using a razor blade or a sharp knife, score the bread. I love baking my bread in a cast iron pot – it traps the moisture and gives the bread a beautiful crust. Use the edges of the baking parchment to transfer the loaf into the pot, if you have one, and pop the lid on. If you don't have a pot, simply transfer the loaf, on its parchment, to a heavy baking tray.

Put your bread in the oven and, if you are not using a pot with a lid, carefully place a bowl of boiling water at the base. Close the door quickly to catch the steam generated. Bake for 40 minutes or until the bread is golden brown and sounds hollow when tapped on the bottom.

Although it's very tempting to eat straight away, allow your bread to cool completely before slicing. The baked loaf can be frozen for later in the week, or for up to 6 months.

Super-soft dinner rolls

 30 minutes + proving   20 minutes   9 rolls   🪙 1

100g/3½oz/scant ½ cup lukewarm
milk
5g/⅛oz/1 tsp fast action dried
yeast
250g/9oz/1¾ cups strong white
bread flour, plus extra for
dusting
1 large egg (63g/2¼oz)
35g/1¼oz/3 tbsp caster
(superfine) sugar
½ tsp salt
45g/1½oz/3 tbsp butter

For finishing
1 egg
1 tbsp milk
1 tbsp butter, melted

+ tip
If you don't have a
square baking tin the
right size, feel free
to bake them in any
other similar-sized
round mould, skillet,
or ovenproof dish.

+ thrifty
Don't throw away your
remaining egg wash!
You can make a nice
little omelette out of it
with leftovers from the
fridge, or freeze in an
ice cube tray to use for
later bakes.

Dinner rolls are one of my go-to breads, especially around wintertime. They're cheap, easy to whip up, and you can make them as simple or as elaborate as you want. Fill them with anything you choose prior to baking: stuff them with a mix of cheese, herbs and garlic; with chocolate spreads or jam; or you can even make a tasty tear-and-share by nestling the dough around some Camembert cheese.

In a large mixing bowl or the bowl of a stand mixer, combine the milk, yeast and 2 tablespoons of the bread flour. Mix together, then leave to stand for 10 minutes.

After this time, add the remaining flour, along with the egg, sugar and salt and mix until combined. If using a stand mixer, add the butter and mix at medium speed for 5 minutes. Or, if making by hand, add the butter to the dough and bring together. Turn the dough out onto a floured work surface and knead until smooth and elastic – about 10 minutes.

Shape the dough into a ball, place in a bowl and cover with a tea towel or cling film (plastic wrap). Leave in a warm place until the dough has doubled in size (about an hour). If you are in a hurry, put the dough in the oven (with the power off) and place a bowl of steaming hot water on the base of the oven. The dough should double in size in about 30 minutes.

Punch the air out of the dough and turn it out onto a work surface. Divide into nine equal pieces and shape them into balls. At this point you can stuff your dough with cheese, chocolate spread or any other fillings of your choice, if you wish.

Grease a 20cm/8in square baking tin with butter. Place the dough balls in the tin, cover them with a clean tea towel and leave them until they have doubled in size – about 1 hour in a warm place or less if you are using the hot water technique above.

Preheat your oven to 180°C/160°C fan/350°F/Gas 4 (removing the bowl of water if necessary).

Just before baking, whisk the extra egg and milk together and brush it over the top of the risen dough. Bake the rolls for 15–20 minutes, or until golden brown on top. Remove from the oven and, while still hot, brush them with the extra butter.

Once cold, wrap the rolls in foil and keep at room temperature for up to 5 days or, if freezing, place them in a freezer bag or airtight container and freeze for up to 1 month.

Ham and cheese brioche rolls

 40 minutes + proving   20 minutes   6 rolls   3

3 large eggs

about 50g/1¾oz/3½ tbsp milk
(see method)

350g/12oz/2½ cups strong white
bread flour, plus extra for
dusting

60g/2oz/5 tbsp caster (superfine)
sugar

10g/⅓oz/2 tsp fast action dried
yeast

5g/⅛oz/1 tsp salt

170g/6oz/¾ cup butter, cubed
and at room temperature

For the filling

150g/5½oz smoked ham, diced

100g/3½oz Gruyère cheese, finely
grated

2 tbsp chopped parsley

½ tsp smoked paprika

freshly ground black pepper

For glazing

1 egg

1 tbsp milk

+ thrifty

I've used Gruyère cheese
because its sweet, nutty
flavour complements
any bread and cured
meat combination. But
it can be pricey, so you
can use any hard cheese
but remember: the
stronger the cheese, the
less you will need. You
can also use any leftover
eggwash you may have
saved in the freezer.

Brioche was my first attempt to make bread and it's always a hit
wherever I take it. This recipe is a savoury variation of my blueberry
buns (see page 38), making use of the last couple of ham slices in
the fridge and the end of the cheese block, plus a few herbs.

When it comes to baking, you can make something very simple
look more interesting when you present it well. I decided to plait
and knot these rolls to create beautiful intricate-looking curves –
something you could be really proud of putting on the table.

Place a bowl on the scales and set it to zero, then crack in your
eggs. Add enough milk to bring the combined weight to 210g/7½oz.

In your stand mixer bowl, combine the flour, sugar, yeast, salt and
the egg and milk mixture. Mix on slow speed for a minute or so until
everything is roughly combined, then on medium-high for about
5 minutes. Now start adding the butter pieces gradually, mixing in
each piece before you add the next, until it's all well incorporated
and your dough looks silky.

Cover the bowl and refrigerate for 4–5 hours, or until the dough is
firm enough to shape. Ideally leave your dough to ferment in the
fridge overnight – this allows it to develop its flavour.

The next day, line a baking tray with baking parchment. Roll out
the dough on a flour-dusted surface to a rectangle measuring 36
x 40cm/14 x 16in and arrange it with a short edge in front of you.
Sprinkle the ham, cheese, parsley, paprika and black pepper over
the top half of the rectangle, then fold up the uncovered bottom half
to form a 36 x 20cm/14 x 8in rectangle.

Using a knife, slice the dough vertically into six equal strips, each
measuring 6 x 20cm/2½ x 8in. Select a strip and make two more
vertical cuts so that the strip is in three long strands, but leave
1cm/½in uncut at the top to hold the strands together. Plait these
three strands together, then, starting from the end you'll still be
holding, roll up the plait back onto itself like a narrow Swiss roll.
Place the roll on the prepared tray with the seam side down and
repeat to shape the other five rolls, placing them on the tray as
you go and allowing space around them for the dough to expand.
Leave to prove for 4–5 hours at room temperature, or until the
dough is puffy and has almost, but not quite, doubled in size. Over
proving the dough will affect the intricate design.

Preheat the oven to 190°C/170°C fan/375°F/Gas 5. Beat the extra
egg and milk together to make an egg wash and brush it over the
rolls. Bake for 20 minutes or until golden brown. Enjoy warm.

Hotdog pretzels

 30 minutes + proving 15 minutes 12 pretzels 1

90g/3¼oz/6 tbsp lukewarm water

90g/3¼oz/6 tbsp lukewarm milk

5g/⅛oz/1 tsp fast action dried yeast

300g/10½oz/2¼ cups strong white bread flour, plus optional extra for dusting

15g/½oz/4 tsp caster (superfine) sugar

5g/⅛oz/1 tsp salt

30g/1oz/2 tbsp butter

oil, for greasing

12 hotdog sausages

670g/23oz/scant 3 cups water, for boiling the pretzels

21g/¾oz/1½ tbsp bicarbonate of soda (baking soda)

1 egg

1 tbsp milk

grated cheese, nigella seeds or sesame seeds (optional)

+ tip

To make sweet pretzels:

If you have any leftover ropes of dough, cut them into 2–3cm/¾–1¼in pieces. Dunk them in the water bath, then bake as you would in the recipe above, giving them a little less time in the oven. To finish, mix together **1 teaspoon ground cinnamon per 2 tablespoons caster (superfine) sugar**. Brush the cooked pretzel bites generously with **melted butter**, then sprinkle with the cinnamon sugar and serve.

I absolutely love pretzels; they make a great snack and are very versatile. You can use meat-free, chicken or beef hotdogs – the choice really is yours. Pack sizes vary, so if you don't have 12 in your pack, you'll have too much dough. We waste nothing, so my tip explains how to turn leftover dough into sweet pretzel bites.

Serve the pretzels with sides such as mustard, ketchup and onions browned in butter.

In a large mixing bowl or stand mixer bowl, combine the warm water and milk, add the yeast and allow to sit for 5 minutes.

Add the flour, sugar and salt to the bowl and mix until combined. If hand kneading, add the butter to the dough and bring together, then turn the dough out onto a flour-dusted surface and knead until smooth and elastic – about 10 minutes. If using a stand mixer, attach the dough hook, then add the butter and mix at medium speed for about 5 minutes, or until the dough is smooth and pulls away from the sides of the bowl.

Shape the dough into a ball. Grease a clean bowl with a little oil, place the dough in it and cover with a towel or some cling film (plastic wrap). Leave in a warm place until the dough has doubled in size – about 1 hour. Meanwhile, preheat your oven to 200°C/180°C fan/400°F/Gas 6 and line a baking tray with baking parchment.

Once proved, punch the air out of the dough and turn it onto a work surface. Cut the dough into 12 equal pieces, then stretch and roll each piece into a 30cm/12in long rope. Wrap each rope in a spiral around a hotdog sausage.

Prepare a soda water bath by putting the water for boiling in a saucepan and adding the bicarbonate of soda (which should be 3 per cent of the weight of the water). Bring to the boil. Using a spider or slotted spoon and working with just one or two at a time, dip each pretzel hotdog into the boiling soda water for 20 seconds. Once dunked, transfer each one to the lined baking tray.

Beat together the egg and milk to make an egg wash, then brush the pretzel hotdogs with it. If liked, you can now sprinkle over some grated cheese, or nigella or sesame seeds, if you have them.

Bake for about 15 minutes, or until all the pretzels are golden brown. Allow them to cool slightly before serving warm.

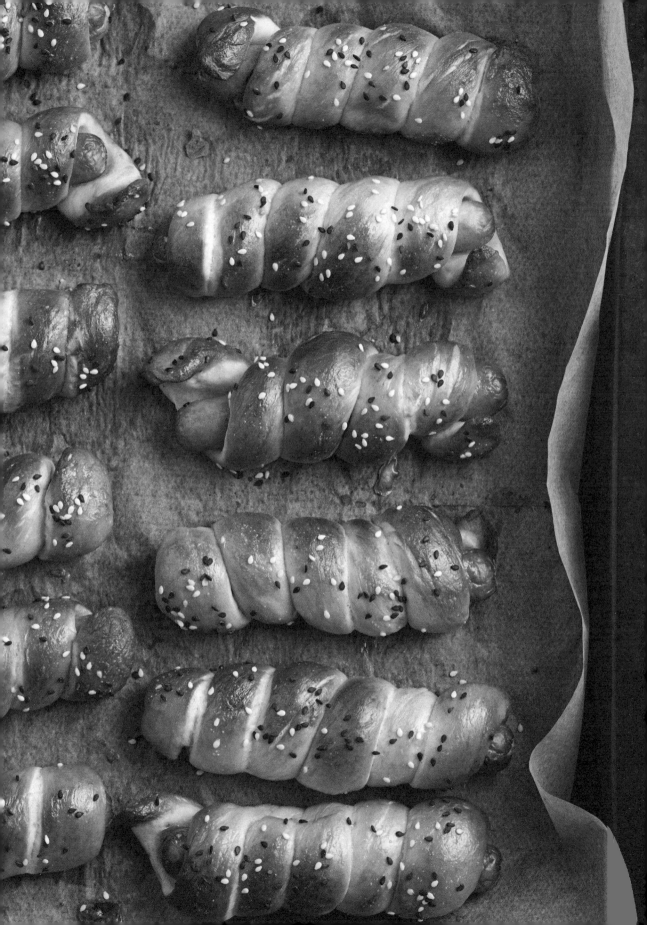

Cinnamon rolls

 40 minutes + proving   25 minutes   🍴 12 rolls   1

2 large eggs
about 40g/1½oz/2½ tbsp whole
    milk (see method)
250g/9oz/1¾ cups strong white
    bread flour
50g/1¾oz/¼ cup caster
    (superfine) sugar
10g/⅓oz/2 tsp fast action dried
    yeast
½ tsp salt
120g/4¼oz/½ cup unsalted butter,
    at room temperature

To finish

150g/5½oz/¾ cup caster
    (superfine) sugar
1 tsp ground cinnamon
80g/2¾oz/⅓ cup unsalted butter,
    softened, plus extra for greasing
1 egg
1 tbsp milk

I've made a few cinnamon rolls in my time but came across this recipe by pure chance. I made a brioche dough that ended up spending 48 hours in the fridge before I found time to shape it. That morning, I decided to turn the dough into some cinnamon rolls and just could not believe how incredibly delicious they were!

You can add a glaze or some cream cheese frosting, but I promise you these rolls are gorgeous just the way they are. When I first made them at home, we ate the lot within the hour.

Place a bowl on the scales and set it to zero, then crack in your eggs. Add enough milk to bring the combined weight to 150g/5½oz.

In your stand mixer bowl, combine the flour, sugar, yeast, salt and the egg and milk mixture. Mix on slow speed for a minute or so until everything is roughly combined, then on medium-high for about 5 minutes. Now start adding the butter pieces gradually, mixing in each piece before you add the next, until it's all well incorporated and your dough looks silky.

Cover the bowl and chill overnight to develop the flavour. For a quicker turnaround, sit the bowl in a warm place for about an hour until your dough has doubled in size, then refrigerate it for a further hour (this step is not compulsory but will make it easier for you to roll out, cut and shape your dough).

When ready to proceed, mix the cinnamon and sugar together, then set aside one-third of it to use for the moulds and topping.

Choose what you're going to bake the cinnamon rolls in: you can use a 33 x 23cm/13 x 9in baking tin; a 23cm/9in round cake tin; a skillet; or a 12-hole muffin tin. Grease the tin and dust the inside with 1 tablespoon of cinnamon sugar, or 2 tablespoons if you are using muffin tins. This will give your rolls a delicious caramelised base.

On a lightly-floured surface, roll out the dough to a 40 x 30cm/16 x 12in sheet. Spread evenly with the soft butter, then sprinkle over the remaining cinnamon sugar. Starting from a long edge of the rectangle, roll up the dough and cut it into 12 equal pieces. Arrange the cinnamon rolls in the prepared tin, then cover and leave to prove in a warm place for about an hour, or until doubled in size.

When almost ready to bake, preheat the oven to 200°C/180°C fan/400°F/Gas 6. Beat the extra egg and milk together and brush the cinnamon rolls lightly with egg wash. Bake for 20–25 minutes or until lightly browned. Remove from the oven and sprinkle over the remaining cinnamon sugar. Enjoy warm.

Blueberry and custard brioche buns

 1 hour + proving   20 minutes | 6 buns   3

3 large eggs
about 50g/1¾oz/3½ tbsp whole
   milk (see method)
350g/12oz/2½ cups strong white
   bread flour
70g/2½oz/⅓ cup plus 1 tsp caster
   (superfine) sugar
10g/⅓oz/1 tbsp fast action dried
   yeast
5g/⅛oz/1 tsp salt
170g/6oz/¾ cup unsalted butter,
   at room temperature, cubed

For the crème pâtissière
300g/10½oz/1¼ cups whole milk
3 large egg yolks
1 tsp vanilla extract
50g/1¾oz/¼ cup caster
   (superfine) sugar
¼ tsp salt
25g/1oz/¼ cup cornflour
   (cornstarch)
15g/½oz/1 tbsp unsalted butter

For the crumble
150g/5½oz/1 cup plus 2 tbsp plain
   (all-purpose) flour
70g/2½oz/⅓ cup plus 1 tsp caster
   (superfine) sugar
100g/3½oz/scant ½ cup unsalted
   butter, cubed
1 tsp vanilla extract
½ tsp salt

For the blueberries
300g/10½oz/2¼ cups blueberries
2 tbsp sugar

For the egg wash
1 egg yolk
1 tbsp milk

+ tip
Ideally, prove the dough
in the fridge overnight,
which will develop its
flavour.

Buttery, flaky brioche is my signature bake, but I have upgraded
it over the years, adding custard and blueberries when in season.

First, get the dough started. Place a bowl on the scales and set
it to zero, then crack in your eggs. Add enough milk to bring the
combined weight to 210g/7½oz.

In your stand mixer bowl, stir together the flour, sugar, yeast, salt
and the egg and milk mixture. Using the dough hook, mix slowly to
roughly combine everything, then increase the speed to medium-
high and mix for about 5 minutes. Now start adding the butter
pieces gradually, mixing in each piece before you add the next,
until it's all incorporated and your dough is silky. Cover the bowl and
refrigerate for 4–5 hours, or until the dough is firm enough to shape.

Meanwhile, make the crème pâtissière. Bring the milk to scalding
point in a saucepan. In a mixing bowl, whisk together the egg yolks,
vanilla, sugar and salt. Add the cornflour and mix well. Temper the
egg mixture by slowly pouring the hot milk over it while whisking
continuously. Return the custard to the pan and stir until thickened,
then add the butter and mix until incorporated. Transfer to a bowl,
cover the surface with cling film and place in the fridge to cool.

For the crumble, combine the flour, sugar, butter, vanilla and salt
in a small bowl. Using the tips of your fingers, rub the ingredients
together until the mixture has a crumbly texture. Set aside.

Cook half the blueberries with the sugar in a small saucepan over
medium–low heat until they are softened and mushy, then set aside
to cool. Line a baking sheet with baking parchment.

Once it has proved, remove the dough from the refrigerator and
turn it onto a floured surface. Cut the dough into six equal portions
and shape each one into a ball. Using a rolling pin, roll each ball
into a 10cm/4in disc. Use your fingertips to create a deep dip in
the centre of each disc to accommodate the filling. Put the discs
on the baking sheet, cover with a clean tea towel and allow to
prove at room temperature for 3–4 hours or until the dough is puffy
and almost doubled in size. Towards the end of the proving time,
preheat the oven to 200°C/fan 180°C/400°F/Gas 6.

Fill the centre of each bun with a generous tablespoon of the crème
pâtissière. Top with a teaspoon of the cooked blueberries and finish
with a few fresh berries. Make an egg wash by whisking the egg
yolk and milk together, then brush it over the outer rims of the buns.
Sprinkle some crumble over the buns, then bake for 20 minutes or
until golden brown. Serve warm.

Sardine soda bread

 30 minutes  30 minutes 1 loaf 1

1 x 125g/4½oz can sardines in sunflower oil, drained and oil reserved

1 small–medium onion, finely chopped (about 100g/3½oz prepared weight)

½ tsp garlic powder

¼ tsp ground black pepper

100g/3½oz fresh tomatoes, finely diced

200g/7oz/1½ cups plain (all-purpose) flour (gf plus ½ tsp xanthan gum), plus extra for dusting

60g/2oz/scant ½ cup wholemeal flour (gf)

½ tsp bicarbonate of soda (baking soda)

½ tsp baking powder (gf)

40g/1½oz/⅓ cup rolled or porridge oats (gf)

½ tsp salt

40g/1½oz/2 tbsp plus 2 tsp cold unsalted butter, cubed

50g/1¾oz/3½ tbsp buttermilk (or see tip)

1 large egg

15g/½oz/1 tbsp plus 1 tsp sugar (or 1 tbsp clear honey)

10g/⅓oz/2½ tbsp flat-leaf parsley, chopped

I love sardines – they are cheap and full of good micronutrients. If you like them too, you won't be disappointed with this soda bread. It's gorgeous served with a slab of butter.

Growing up, we ate small parcels of deep-fried bread dough filled with caramelised onions, tomatoes and sardines. We called them 'paté', and anywhere they were, you would find me! Which is why I was keen to replicate their flavours in this recipe.

The ingredients here are all store-cupboard items. I've included wholemeal flour and porridge oats to add bit of complexity, but if you don't have any, feel free to substitute them with plain (all-purpose) flour. Fish also goes well with herbs like chives and dill, so if you have either of those to hand, use them instead of parsley.

In a small saucepan over medium heat, combine the oil from the sardine can with the onion, garlic powder and black pepper. Cook, stirring, until the onion softens and starts to caramelise. Add the tomatoes and allow them to simmer and reduce for a minute or so. Set aside to cool.

Heat the oven to 220°C/200°C fan/425°F/Gas 7 and line a baking sheet with baking parchment.

Sift the flours, bicarbonate of soda and baking powder into a mixing bowl to get rid of any lumps and aerate the flour. Add the oats, salt and butter and rub the butter into the dry ingredients using your fingertips, until you have a crumbly texture.

In a separate bowl, lightly beat the buttermilk, egg and sugar together. Add this liquid to the flour mixture, then crumble in the sardines and add the cooled onions and parsley. Mix well to bring the dough together, being careful not to overwork it.

Tip the dough onto a lightly floured surface and bring together into a round (boule). Put it on the prepared baking sheet, cut a deep cross into the top of the loaf and bake for 30 minutes, or until golden brown.

Soda bread tends to dry out quickly, so if you can't consume it all within the next couple of days, it is a good idea to cut only what you need, place the rest in an airtight freezer bag and freeze for up to 3 months.

+ thrifty

If you don't have any buttermilk, you can substitute with 45g/1½oz/3 tbsp milk mixed with 5g/⅛oz/1 tsp vinegar or lemon juice.

Butternut squash curry buns

 30 minutes + proving   20 minutes   12 buns   1

100g/3½oz/scant ½ cup lukewarm
   milk
10g/⅓oz/2 tsp fast action dried
   yeast
500g/1lb 2oz/3⅔ cups strong
   white bread flour, plus optional
   extra for dusting (if kneading by
   hand)
60g/2oz/5 tbsp caster
   (superfine) sugar
200g/7oz mashed roasted
   butternut squash (see page 44),
   or canned pumpkin purée
2 large eggs
10g/⅓oz/2 tsp salt
80g/2¾oz/⅓ cup butter, at room
   temperature

For the curry

2 tbsp sunflower oil
1 medium onion, diced
2 garlic cloves, finely chopped
2 tsp curry powder
½ tsp garam masala
½ tsp ground ginger
150g/5½oz skinless, boneless
   chicken thighs, cut into 1cm/½in
   pieces
1 chicken stock cube
a large handful of fresh coriander
   (cilantro), chopped
½ tsp honey
1 tbsp plain (all-purpose) flour
150g/5½oz diced, roasted
   butternut squash (see page 44)
50g/1¾oz/3½ tbsp canned
   coconut milk
½ tsp salt

To finish

1 egg
1 tbsp milk
sesame or nigella (black onion)
   seeds, to sprinkle (optional)

I don't know about you, but I always have a box in the fridge with some leftover stew, mince, casserole or curry. I find stuffed buns are a great vessel for those leftovers, providing a different take on the humble sandwich.

In case you don't have any leftovers, I'm sharing my simple curry recipe, which features the same butternut squash I use in the chai butternut cake on page 46, so you could roast enough for the two recipes together and save energy (see tip overleaf). You can swap the butternut squash for pumpkin when in season, or use some sweet potatoes or white potatoes instead – although if you do use sweet potatoes, omit the sugar in the bread dough.

I've chosen chicken thighs not only because they are an economical cut, but because they stay moist when cooked, unlike chicken breasts which can dry out quickly.

The curry recipe makes the right amount for one batch of buns, but to save on cooking energy, you could easily double it up so you have another batch ready to go in the freezer (it will freeze for up to 3 months).

For the dough, combine the milk and yeast in a large mixing bowl or stand mixer bowl and allow to stand for 5 minutes. After this time, add the bread flour, sugar, butternut squash purée, eggs and salt and mix until combined.

If hand kneading, add the butter to the dough and bring together. Turn the dough out onto a floured work surface and knead until the dough is smooth and elastic – about 10 minutes. If using a stand mixer, add the butter and mix at medium speed for 5 minutes.

Shape the dough into a ball, place in a bowl and cover with a tea towel or some cling film (plastic wrap). Leave in a warm place until the dough has doubled in size – about 1 hour. Meanwhile, line a baking sheet with baking parchment.

While the dough is proving, make the curry. Heat the oil in a saucepan on medium heat. Add the onion, garlic and all the dried spices and fry for 8–10 minutes or until the onion is soft and brown. Add the chicken and cook, stirring, for about 5 minutes.

Crumble in the stock cube and add the coriander and honey. Stir in the cornflour, then add the roasted butternut squash, coconut milk and salt. Bring to a simmer and leave to cook for a few minutes – you want a thick stew that you can easily spoon into the dough once cold. Set aside to cool.

To roast butternut squash: I always try and roast my squash while something else is in the oven, as it can cook on a tray on a lower shelf and save energy. Simply peel **a whole butternut squash** and dice it into 2cm/¾in chunks, removing the seeds as you go. Drizzle with **olive oil** and roast for about 30 minutes at 180°C/160°C fan/350°F/Gas 4, stirring halfway through cooking, or until soft and golden.

Punch the air out of the dough and turn it out onto a work surface. Divide the dough into 12 equal pieces. Flatten a piece and put a tablespoon of chicken curry at the centre of each. Gather up and join the edges of the dough – pressing the edges together and giving them a little twist to seal – to enclose the filling, then shape into a ball and sit the buns on the prepared baking sheet with the seams underneath.

Leave the buns to rise for about an hour in a warm place, until they have doubled in size. If it is cold in your kitchen, this may take longer. To speed up the process, you can place your buns in the oven without switching it on and sit a bowl of steaming-hot water at the base of the oven.

Preheat the oven to 200°C/180°C fan/400°F/Gas 6, removing the tray of buns and bowl of water if necessary.

Prepare the egg wash by beating the egg and milk together. Brush this over the buns and sprinkle with sesame or nigella seeds, if using. Bake for about 20 minutes or until golden brown. Allow the buns to cool slightly, then enjoy them warm.

These go a little stale if stored in the fridge, so if you don't need them all, it's best to store them in the freezer (wrapped well, and for up to 3 months) and thaw when required. Reheat a batch of them in the oven for 20 minutes, or in an air fryer, or reheat single ones for a few seconds in the microwave.

Cakes for Tea

Chai butternut cake

 30 minutes 30–40 minutes 12 1

100g/3½oz/scant ½ cup vegetable oil, plus extra for greasing

150g/5½oz/1 cup plus 2 tbsp plain (all-purpose) flour, plus extra for flouring

1 tsp baking powder

½ tsp bicarbonate of soda (baking soda)

2 tsp ground cinnamon, plus extra for decoration

½ tsp ground ginger

½ tsp ground nutmeg

¼ tsp ground allspice

¼ tsp ground cloves

½ tsp salt

180g/6¼oz roasted butternut squash, mashed (see page 44)

150g/5½oz/¾ cup caster (superfine) sugar

2 large eggs

1 tsp vanilla extract

For the frosting

100g/3½oz/scant ½ cup unsalted butter, at room temperature

100g/3½oz/¾ cup icing (confectioners') sugar

a pinch of salt

1 tsp espresso powder

1 tsp hot water

100g/3½oz/scant ½ cup cream cheese

1 tsp vanilla bean paste or vanilla extract

+ tip

I love the look of this baked in a 900g/2lb loaf tin, but as it's much deeper, it will take 50 minutes to 1 hour to cook, and therefore use more energy.

A 'kill two birds (or maybe five) with one stone' recipe. Roast cubes of butternut squash (or even a pumpkin) and use some as a side dish, some to make a soup or curry, some for buns (see page 43) and the rest for this delicious cake. Perfect for the colder months, it's made with spices found in most kitchens and will fill your heart with warmth. You could add some chocolate chunks if you have any, but I am keeping mine simple.

Preheat the oven to 180°C/160°C fan/350°F/Gas 4. Grease and flour a 20cm/8in square tin or a 23cm/9in round tin.

In a medium-sized bowl, mix together the flour, baking powder, bicarbonate of soda, ground spices and salt, and set aside.

In a large bowl, combine the vegetable oil, mashed butternut squash, sugar, eggs and vanilla and mix until well combined. Stir the dry ingredients into the wet ingredients and mix thoroughly.

Pour the batter into the prepared tin and bake for 30 minutes, until a skewer inserted into the centre comes out clean. Remove from the oven and set aside to cool completely in the tin.

While the cake is cooling, make the frosting. In a mixing bowl, cream together the butter, icing sugar and salt until light and fluffy.

In a separate bowl, dissolve the espresso powder in the hot water. Add the cream cheese and stir until smooth and well combined. Add the coffee cheese mixture to the buttercream, along with the vanilla, and mix thoroughly.

Put your frosting in a piping bag fitted with a St-Honoré nozzle. If you don't have one, cut the end off a disposable piping bag at an angle to give a 1.5cm/⅝in hole, then make a straight 5mm/¼in cut at the tip.

Once your cake is completely cool, pipe diagonal lines of the frosting across the top to cover it, then dust with a tiny bit of cinnamon for colour.

This cake is best eaten on the day it is made, but if you would like to keep it, store in the fridge for up to 5 days. If you have chilled it, let it return to room temperature before serving.

Custard, lemon and thyme honey cake

 1½ hours, plus chilling   30 minutes   8   1

130g/4½oz/½ cup plus 1 tbsp
butter
150g/5½oz/½ cup clear honey,
plus 1 tbsp to glaze
2 large eggs
60g/2oz/5 tbsp caster (superfine)
sugar
finely grated zest of 1 lemon
1 tsp thyme leaves, finely chopped
1 tsp vanilla extract
½ tsp salt
150g/5½oz/1 cup plus 2 tbsp plain
(all-purpose) flour (gf plus ¼ tsp
xanthan gum)
1½ tsp baking powder (gf)

For the crème pâtissière
200g/7oz/scant 1 cup whole milk
small bunch of thyme, about
30g/1oz
2 egg yolks
40g/1½oz/3¼ tbsp caster
(superfine) sugar
1 tsp vanilla extract
a pinch of salt
15g/½oz/2 tbsp cornflour
(cornstarch)
10g/⅓oz/2 tsp butter

+ tip

When crème pâtissière
is cooked, it should be
thick, stiff and smooth,
and clinging to the whisk,
but still soft enough to
spread or pipe.
   To boost the colour of
your crème pâtissière,
choose eggs with
golden yolks, or replace
1 teaspoon of the
cornflour with 1 teaspoon
of custard powder.

When it comes to seasoning, thyme is a must-have. My mother used it a lot and it's no surprise I always have a pot growing by my kitchen window. Here, it pairs beautifully with lemon and honey.

There is a perception that honey can be expensive, but unless you intend to eat it raw or are making a delicate dessert that requires a flower honey, I would just use a low-cost value brand. The cake is delicious on its own, and can be served warm straight from the oven, so you really could just make the honey sponge, but I like to elevate it a notch with a thyme-infused crème pâtissière.

Make the crème pâtissière at least a couple of hours in advance, so it has time to set firm. Put the milk and thyme in a small saucepan over a low heat and bring gently to a simmer. Turn off the heat and leave to infuse for about 10 minutes.

Meanwhile, in a medium bowl, whisk together the egg yolks, sugar, vanilla and salt until light and creamy – about 2 minutes. Add the cornflour and mix until combined.

Strain the infused milk through a sieve, then pour it over the egg yolk mixture in a slow, steady stream, mixing continuously. Clean the saucepan and return the custard mixture to it. Place it back over a low heat and stir the mixture continuously until it thickens (see tip, left), then add the butter and mix until fully incorporated. Pour the crème pâtissière into a a small bowl, covering the surface with cling film (plastic wrap) and chill until set.

Preheat the oven to 180°C/160°C fan/350°F/Gas 4. Grease a 20cm/8in round cake tin and line with baking parchment.

To make the honey sponge, melt the butter and honey together in the microwave for about 30 seconds. In a separate mixing bowl, whisk the eggs and sugar together until light and fluffy. Add the honey–butter mixture, plus the lemon zest, thyme, vanilla and salt and mix until well combined. Stir in the flour and baking powder until combined. Pour the batter into the prepared tin and bake for 30 minutes, or until the cake is golden brown and a skewer inserted into the centre comes out clean. Turn the cake out onto a wire rack and allow to cool completely.

Once cool, slice the cake horizontally in half, fill with a generous layer of your crème pâtissière, and top with the second layer of cake. Melt the honey for glazing for a few seconds in the microwave, then brush it over the top of the cake with a pastry brush to give it a lovely shine. Chill until you are almost ready to serve, then leave the cake at room temperature for 30 minutes before slicing.

Chocolate torte cake

 1 hour  40 minutes 12 1

90g/3¼oz dark (bittersweet) chocolate

90g/3¼oz/6 tbsp butter, plus extra for greasing

80g/2¾oz/½ cup plus 1 tbsp icing (confectioners') sugar

1 tsp vanilla bean paste or vanilla extract

¼ tsp salt

4 eggs, separated

70g/2½oz/⅓ cup caster (superfine) sugar

80g/2¾oz/⅔ cup less 1 tbsp plain (all-purpose) flour (*gf plus ¼ tsp xanthan gum*), sifted

200g/7oz/⅔ cup apricot jam, or any other jam of your choice

For the glaze

200g/7oz dark (bittersweet) chocolate, chopped

100g/3½oz/½ cup less 1 tbsp butter

½ tsp instant coffee powder

+ tip

Chocolate works incredibly well with berries, pineapple, peaches, oranges and mangoes, so fill your sponge with any of those jams. You can also go for less traditional fillings such as sweet peanut butter, salted caramel sauce or chocolate hazelnut spread. Use flavours that you like and are already available in your pantry.

This is a chocolate lover's cake: a super-light chocolate sponge filled with a layer of apricot jam and glazed with chocolate. It can double as a tea cake or a celebration cake.

If you're not a fan of apricot, or want to use what you already have, see my tip below for alternative fillings.

Preheat the oven to 200°C/180°C fan/400°F/Gas 6. Grease a 23cm/ 9in cake tin and line with baking parchment.

To make the sponge, melt the chocolate in a heatproof bowl set over a pan of simmering water, or in the microwave for 20 seconds at a time, stirring in between bursts. Set aside to cool.

In a large mixing bowl, cream the butter, icing sugar, vanilla and salt together until light and fluffy. Add the egg yolks one at a time and mix until well combined. Stir in the melted chocolate.

In a stand mixer, or in a mixing bowl and using an electric hand whisk, whisk the egg whites on high speed, adding the caster sugar gradually until the whites reach stiff peak stage.

A little at a time, fold the egg whites into the chocolate mixture, then fold in the flour in small batches. When fully incorporated, pour the batter into the cake tin. Bake for 40 minutes, or until a skewer inserted into the centre of the cake comes out clean. Remove the cake from the oven, gently unmould it from the tin and leave on a wire rack to cool completely – about 1 hour.

Slice the cooled cake in half horizontally. Spread three-quarters of the jam onto the base layer of cake and top with the second layer of the cake. Melt the remaining jam in the microwave in 10–20 second bursts until runny. Brush it over the top and sides of the cake, then leave to set in the fridge for 30 minutes.

To make the chocolate glaze, melt the chocolate, butter and coffee together in a bain marie or in the microwave, as above. Stir until smooth. Allow your glaze to cool a little, but make sure it's still warm.

To avoid wasting any of the glaze, line the kitchen counter with some cling film (plastic wrap) and place your cake on a wire rack over it. Pour the glaze over the cake, making sure it covers the entire cake – use a spatula to gently push the glaze to the edges. Collect any glaze that drips onto the cling film and tip it into a piping bag. Cut a small (1mm/1/32in) hole at the tip of the bag and pipe some decorations onto the cake, such as 's' shapes. Leave the cake at room temperature until the chocolate sets, then it's ready to enjoy.

Orange drizzle cake

 20 minutes 30 minutes 12 1

180g/6¼oz/¾ cup plus 2 tsp
   butter, at room temperature
180g/6¼oz/1¼ cups icing
   (confectioners') sugar
3 eggs
180g/6¼oz/1⅓ cups plain
   (all-purpose) flour (gf plus
   ¼ tsp xanthan gum)
1½ tsp baking powder (gf)
finely grated zest of 2 large
   oranges, plus 200g/7oz/¾ cup
   plus 2 tbsp squeezed juice
½ tsp salt
100g/3½oz/½ cup caster
   (superfine) sugar

Fruits are a great way to add natural flavours to your bake and make use of the last few fruits in the bowl. Orange drizzle cake is deliciously light and moist, and much mellower in taste than lemon drizzle. If you're partial to citrusy flavours, you'll absolutely love this.

Chocolate goes very well with orange, so feel free to add some chocolate chunks to the batter. If you've tried my chocolate chip cookies on page 85, you should be left with a few that will come in handy here if you haven't decided to eat them all! If you do add the chocolate chunks, I would omit the drizzle.

- -

Preheat the oven to 180°C/160°C fan/350°F/Gas 4. Grease a 22cm/8½in round cake tin and line with baking parchment.

In a mixing bowl, cream together the butter and icing sugar until light and fluffy. Add the eggs one at a time, mixing well after each addition. Add the flour, baking powder, orange zest and salt, and mix until just combined. Stir in 50g/1¾oz/3½ tablespoons of the orange juice. (If you're using chocolate chunks, add them now.)

Pour the cake batter into the prepared tin and smooth the surface. Bake for 30 minutes, or until the cake is golden brown and a skewer inserted into the centre comes out clean.

Meanwhile, in a small saucepan, combine the caster sugar and the remaining orange juice. Bring to a boil, then set aside.

Remove your cake from the oven. While it's still hot and in the tin, poke a few holes in the sponge with a bamboo skewer or similar. Using a spoon or a brush, drizzle the syrup all over the cake and let it soak in. Allow the cake to cool before serving.

French apple cake

 30 minutes  30 minutes 12 1

3 apples, any type
juice of ½ lemon (optional)
150g/5½oz/⅔ cup butter, at room temperature, plus 1 tbsp for glazing
150g/5½oz/¾ cup caster (superfine) sugar, plus 1 tbsp for glazing
2 large eggs
100g/3½oz/1 cup ground almonds
1 tsp vanilla extract
¼ tsp salt
100g/3½oz/¾ cup self-raising flour (gf)
2 tbsp rum (optional)
almond flakes (optional)

Here's a delicious moist cake that can be put together quickly at the weekend when the kids are at home and you want to use up those few apples left in the fruit bowl. I often make it when I want a nice cake for afternoon tea or something inexpensive to take round to a friend's house.

I'm using three sliced, halved apples because I like the way it looks, but you can make this cake even with just one apple. In that case, you will need to cut the apple into chunks and fold it into the batter. The lemon juice helps prevent your apples turning brown, but if this is just a cake to devour at home, it is optional, and you need not worry about it.

Ground almonds lend moisture to the cake but if you don't have any, simply substitute self-raising flour. The rum adds a lovely touch but is not compulsory – or you can use brandy, if you have that.

Preheat the oven to 200°C/180°C fan/400°F/Gas 6. Grease and line a 23cm/9in loose-based cake tin with baking parchment.

Use an apple corer to remove the cores of the apples, then peel and cut them in half vertically. Place an apple half, cut-side down, on the chopping board and slice deeply at 4mm/⅛in intervals but without going all the way down to the board so the slices are still attached at the base and the apple half remains in one piece. Squeeze over the lemon juice, if using, to prevent the apple turning brown and set aside while you repeat with the other halves.

In a large mixing bowl, cream together the butter and sugar for about 2 minutes, or until light and fluffy. Add the eggs one at a time, mixing after each addition until well incorporated. Add the ground almonds, vanilla and salt, mix well, then add the flour, taking care not to overmix. Fold in the rum, if using.

Pour the batter into the prepared cake tin and spread it level. Arrange the apple halves on top of the batter with the sliced (rounded) side up. Melt the extra tablespoon of butter and brush it over the fruit. Sprinkle the entire cake with the extra tablespoon of sugar, then scatter the almond flakes over, if using.

Bake for 30 minutes, or until the cake is risen and golden brown. You can test it by inserting a knife in the centre: it should come out clean. Allow the cake to cool in the tin for a few minutes before turning out on a wire rack.

The cake can be stored in an airtight container for up to 3 days or for a week in the fridge. Microwave a portion for 10 seconds or so to enjoy it warm again.

+ tip
Substitute the caster sugar with golden caster or light brown sugar (see page 16) to add even more depth of flavour to your cake.

Coconut, raspberry and chocolate muffins

 20 minutes 30 minutes 12 muffins  1

180g/6¼oz/¾ cup milk

2 large eggs

60g/2oz/¼ cup vegetable oil

60g/2oz/4 tbsp unsalted butter, melted

230g/8oz/1 cup plus 2 tbsp sugar

1 tsp vanilla extract

½ tsp ground cinnamon

¼ tsp ground nutmeg

5g/⅛oz/1 tsp salt

250g/9oz/heaped 1¾ cups plain (all-purpose) flour (gf plus ½ tsp xanthan gum)

80g/2¾oz/1 cup desiccated (dried shredded) coconut

10g/⅓oz/2 tsp baking powder (gf)

150g/5½oz raspberries

150g/5½oz milk chocolate, chopped into chunks

Denser and not as sweet as cupcakes, muffins make a great breakfast on the go. You can pack them with fruits, nuts or chocolate. The combination here tastes wonderful whether you're using fresh raspberries in season (when they're cheaper) or frozen raspberries.

To enhance the flavour of your desiccated coconut, you could toast it lightly (for 5 minutes or so) while preheating the oven – but keep an eye on it as it does turn brown very quickly.

If you have tried my chocolate chip cookie recipe (see page 85) and have some leftover chocolate, use it here. If you don't have muffin cases on hand, check the equipment section (see pages 10–11) to see how you can make your own using baking parchment – they are what I use at home for these muffins and are so much cheaper than shop-bought tulip cases.

- -

Preheat the oven to 200°C/180°C fan/400°F/Gas 6 and line a 12-hole muffin tin with paper cases.

In a large mixing bowl, mix together the milk, eggs, oil, melted butter, sugar, vanilla, cinnamon, nutmeg and salt for about a minute, until well combined. Add the flour, coconut and baking powder and stir until fully incorporated. Fold in half the raspberries and all the chocolate chunks.

Divide the batter equally between the muffin cases. Top each muffin with a couple of the remaining raspberries. Bake for 25–30 minutes, or until the muffins have risen and are golden brown.

You can keep these for a few days in an airtight container, or, once cooled, freeze them for up to 3 months. They are lovely served warm – either out the oven or reheated for a few seconds in the microwave.

Caramelised upside-down banana and chocolate cake

 30 minutes 45 minutes 12 1

3 small bananas

150g/5½oz/⅔ cup butter

150g/5½oz/¾ cup light brown sugar

¼ tsp salt

3 large eggs

50g/1¾oz/3½ tbsp milk, buttermilk or yoghurt

180g/6¼oz/1⅓ cups plain (all-purpose) flour (gf plus ¼ tsp xanthan gum)

1 tsp baking powder (gf)

½ tsp bicarbonate of soda (baking soda)

½ tsp ground ginger

½ tsp ground cinnamon

50g/1¾oz chocolate, finely chopped, or to taste

1 tsp vanilla bean paste or vanilla extract

For the caramel

20g/⅔oz/4 tsp water

150g/5½oz/¾ cup caster (superfine) sugar

70g/2½oz/⅓ cup less 1 tsp butter

1 tsp vanilla bean paste or vanilla extract

¼ tsp salt

+ tip

When making caramel, it's really important to add the sugar to the water in the pan, not the other way round. Also, adding a few drops of lemon juice to your sugar/water mixture at the start will stop the sugar crystallizing when cooking. Read more about making caramel on page 20.

Bananas are great for baking once soft and mushy. This simple upside-down cake makes a delicious change from banana bread. If you only have a couple of bananas, cut them into disks so that they stretch further to cover the base of your tin. To bring colour to your finished cake, cook the caramel to a rich amber – but at the same time, be careful not to take it too far and burn it. Better an undercooked caramel that makes your cake look a little pale than a burnt one that makes your cake taste bitter.

Preheat your oven to 190°C/170°C fan/375°F/Gas 5. Grease a 23cm/9in round cake tin and line with baking parchment.

First, make the caramel. Put the water in a small saucepan and add the sugar. Cook the sugar and water together until rich amber in colour.

Using a balloon whisk, add the butter to the caramel and whisk until fully incorporated and smooth. Remove from the stove and stir in the vanilla and salt. Once combined, pour the caramel into the prepared cake tin and tilt to make sure it covers the whole base.

Slice your bananas lengthways, each into three long slices, or crossways into small discs. Arrange the banana slices next to each other in the caramel and set the cake tin aside.

Make your cake batter by creaming together the butter, sugar and salt until light and fluffy. Add the eggs one at a time, mixing after each addition, then add the milk, buttermilk or yoghurt and mix until fully incorporated. Sift in the flour, baking powder, bicarbonate of soda, ginger and cinnamon and mix until combined. Finally, fold in the chocolate and vanilla.

Pour the cake batter into the cake tin on top of the bananas and bake for 40–45 minutes, or until a skewer inserted at the centre comes out clean. Remove the cake from the oven and let it sit in the tin for 5 minutes before unmoulding it onto a flat plate and leaving it to cool slightly. Enjoy warm.

The bananas will start to look unpleasant after a while, so best eat this cake within a couple of days.

Basque cake

 1 hour 40 minutes 12 1

For the crème pâtissière

200g/7oz/scant 1 cup whole milk
3 large egg yolks
40g/1½oz/3¼ tbsp caster
   (superfine) sugar
20g/⅔oz/2½ tbsp cornflour
   (cornstarch)
1 tsp vanilla bean paste or vanilla
   extract
a pinch of salt
15g/½oz/1 tbsp butter

For the pastry

250g/9oz/heaped 1¾ cups plain
   (all-purpose) flour, plus extra for
   dusting
160g/5¾oz/¾ cup plus 1 tbsp
   caster (superfine) sugar
15g/½oz/1½ tbsp baking powder
½ tsp salt
finely grated zest of 1 lemon
180g/6¼oz/¾ cup plus 2 tsp
   butter, at room temperature,
   plus extra for greasing
1 large egg, plus 2 egg yolks
1 tsp vanilla bean paste or vanilla
   extract (or any other flavour of
   your choice)

For the egg wash

1 egg yolk
1 tsp milk or double (heavy) cream

+ tip

The addition of custard
powder gives the crème
patissiere a thicker texture
and some added colour.
If you don't have any,
cornflour (cornstarch)
is a great substitute for
thickening, and eggs with
extra-golden yolks will
add some colour.

Imagine a layer of thick crème pâtissière sandwiched between two layers of short pastry with a cakey texture; to me, that is just heaven.

Make this cake your own by filling it with whatever you have on hand: try a layer of jam or chocolate spread in the base before adding the custard; make chocolate-flavoured crème pâtissière; or simply add some fresh berries to the crème pâtissière after piping.

To make the crème pâtissière, bring the milk to scalding point in a medium saucepan. Whisk the egg yolks and sugar together in a bowl. Add the cornflour, vanilla and salt and mix until smooth. Pour in the warm milk in a slow, steady stream while mixing continuously. Return the mixture to the saucepan and stir continuously until the custard thickens. Add the butter and mix well. Pour into a container, cover the surface with cling film (plastic wrap) and refrigerate until firm and cold.

For the pastry, combine the flour, sugar, baking powder, salt and lemon zest in a large bowl. Add the butter and rub in with your fingertips until you have a fine crumble-like texture. Add the egg and egg yolks and the vanilla and mix to a dough. Divide the dough into two equal portions, wrap in cling film and roll each slightly with a rolling pin to form a rough disc about 2.5cm/1in thick. Refrigerate for 40 minutes, or until the pastry is firm and ready to roll easily.

Meanwhile, prepare your egg wash by mixing the ingredients until smooth. Grease and flour a deep 23cm/9in tart or cake tin.

Once the pastry is firm, generously flour your work surface and roll each pastry disc into a circle 23cm/9in wide and about 5mm/¼in thick. Don't worry too much about neat edges so long as the pastry covers the base of your tin. Place the first disc at the bottom of your cake tin. If your dough is too soft to work with, you can chill it again for a few minutes. Pipe or evenly spoon the chilled crème pâtissière over the pastry disc in the tin, leaving a 2.5cm/1in rim at the edge bare. Brush the egg wash around the rim of the pastry. Lay the second pastry disc on top of the crème pâtissière and press around the edge to seal the two discs firmly. Brush the egg wash over the top of the pastry and place in the fridge for 30 minutes.

Once the pastry is chilled, preheat your oven to 220°C/200°C fan/ 425°F/Gas 7. Take the assembled cake from the fridge and give it another brush with the last of the egg wash. Score the pastry with a design of your choice. Lower the oven temperature to 200°C/ 180°C fan/400°F/Gas 6 and bake for 40 minutes, or until golden. Carefully unmould the cake from the tin and allow to cool slightly on a wire rack. Enjoy warm.

Orange and brown butter madeleines

 30 minutes   12 minutes per batch   24 madeleines

180g/6¼oz/¾ cups brown butter (see page 18), made from 220g/7¾oz/1 cup unsalted butter
130g/4½oz/⅔ cup golden caster (superfine) sugar
finely grated zest of 1 small orange
2 large eggs
1 tsp vanilla bean paste
a pinch of salt
40g/1¼oz/2½ tbsp whole milk
40g/1¼oz/2½ tbsp orange juice (from the zested orange)
200g/7oz/1½ cups plain (all-purpose) flour (gf plus ½ tsp xanthan gum), sifted
1½ tsp baking powder (gf)

+ thrifty

Although madeleines are known for their distinctive shape, there is no rule to say that you cannot bake this batter in a mini muffin tin, if that's what you have. Any shallow mini cake tin will fit the assignment; they'll still taste absolutely delicious – there's no need to spend money on a new baking tin.

When baking on a budget, the goal is to achieve maximum flavour with as few ingredients as possible. Brown butter, which is regular butter that has been allowed to reduce and caramelise, is a great way to do this. It has a completely different flavour to normal butter – it's nutty, full of aroma and can really elevate your bake. I always have a jar ready to go in my fridge.

Madeleines are quick to make and are a great addition to packed lunches because, unlike bought packaged cakes, you know exactly what went in them. If you don't have baking powder at home, just replace the plain flour with self-raising flour.

If you're sharing them with adults only, try flavouring your madeleines with alcohol such as rum, brandy or cognac, if you have some at home. You can also use the zest of any citrus fruit – a great way to use up the last in the fruit bowl – or add some chocolate chips to the batter. You can even coat the baked madeleines in chocolate.

- -

Make the brown butter according to the instructions on page 18. Strain the butter through a fine-mesh sieve and set aside to cool completely.

Put the sugar and orange zest together in a large bowl and rub the zest into the sugar with your fingertips to release the orange flavour. Add the eggs, vanilla and salt and, using a whisk or spatula, mix until combined. Pour in the milk, still mixing, then add the orange juice – do not add them together as the acidity of the juice might curdle the milk. Fold in the flour and baking powder.

Working in batches, fold 150g/5½oz of your brown butter (save the rest for greasing the moulds) into the batter until incorporated. Cover the batter and leave it to rest in the fridge for 1½ hours – this solidifies the batter and is essential to achieving the distinctive bulge in the madeleines' shape, created when the cold batter is shocked by the hot oven.

Preheat the oven to 200°C/180°C fan/400°F/Gas mark 6. Grease a 12-hole madeleine mould with half of the reserved brown butter.

Once the batter has chilled, spoon or pipe half of it into the mould, filling the holes about three-quarters full. (Return the remaining batter to the fridge.) Bake for 10–12 minutes, or until risen and golden. Unmould the cakes as soon as they are out of the oven and pop them gently into a bowl, covering with a towel to keep them soft. Repeat to cook the remaining batter.

The madeleines will keep in an airtight container for up to 3 days.

Peach crumble tarte Tropézienne

 1 hour 20 minutes 20 minutes 12 1

1 whole egg (55g/2oz), plus 1 yolk
    for the eggwash
about 70g/1½oz/4½ tbsp whole
    milk (see method), plus 1 tbsp
    for the egg wash
5g/⅛oz/1 tsp fast-action dried
    yeast
200g/7oz/1½ cups strong white
    bread flour
20g/⅔oz/1 tbsp plus 2 tsp caster
    (superfine) sugar
½ tsp salt
60g/2oz/4 tbsp butter, cubed
½ x 400g/14oz can sliced peaches
    (120g/4¼oz drained peaches)

For the crème diplomate

200g/7oz/scant 1 cup whole milk
3 egg yolks
60g/2oz/5 tbsp caster (superfine)
    sugar
1 tsp vanilla bean paste or vanilla
    extract
⅛ tsp salt
10g/⅓oz/1 rounded tbsp plain
    (all-purpose) flour
10g/⅓oz/1 rounded tbsp custard
    powder or cornflour (cornstarch)
1 tbsp brandy (optional)
20g/⅔oz/1½ tbsp butter
200g/7oz/scant 1 cup double
    (heavy) cream

For the crumble

15g/½oz/1¾ tbsp plain
    (all-purpose) flour
15g/½oz/1 tbsp butter
15g/½oz/1 tbsp plus 1 tsp sugar

For the syrup

50g/1¾oz/¼ cup sugar
50g/1¾oz/3½ tbsp water
1 tsp vanilla bean paste or vanilla
    extract

Tarte Tropézienne is a beautiful, elegant bake that you will be very proud to present. It is made of fluffy brioche filled with crème diplomate: a combination of crème pâtissière and chantilly cream.

I will always encourage you to be adventurous with your flavours when baking – try flavours that appeal to you, but also that make use of what is already available. While canned peaches are simple, delicious and budget friendly, there are many combinations you could try. Think about replacing the peaches with fresh raspberries and drizzling with a raspberry coulis, or using strawberries in season, or caramelised apple, or rhubarb. You could even replace the peaches with praline, chocolate or salted caramel.

Adding flavours to the crumble, such as cinnamon, cocoa or citrus zest, is also a great way to experiment with this recipe.

To make the crème diplomate, bring the milk to scalding point in a medium saucepan. In a bowl, whisk the egg yolks, sugar, vanilla and salt together. Add the flour and custard powder or cornflour and mix well.

Temper the egg mixture by slowly pouring the hot milk over it while whisking continuously. Return the custard to the saucepan and stir continuously until it has thickened. Add the brandy, if using, then whisk in the butter until fully incorporated.

Transfer the custard to a bowl, cover the surface with cling film (plastic wrap) and place in the fridge to cool.

For the brioche dough, place a bowl on the scales and set it to zero, then crack in your whole egg and weigh it. You will need the combined weight of milk and eggs to come to 125g/4½oz, so if your egg weighs 55g/2oz, you'll need 70g/2½oz milk – but don't add it yet. Instead, put the weighed milk in a jug and heat in the microwave until it's lukewarm.

Make the brioche dough by hand or in a stand mixer. Put your lukewarm milk in a large mixing bowl (or the bowl of your stand mixer), stir in the yeast and allow to sit for a few minutes.

Add the flour, sugar, egg and salt and knead for about 10 minutes, or until the dough comes together and is no longer sticky. If using a mixer, attach the dough hook and mix for about a minute on slow speed, then increase the speed to medium–high for about 5 minutes.

Add the butter a little at a time, mixing well until each piece has been incorporated before adding the next, until it's all added and you have a silky dough.

Allow the dough to rest, covered with a clean tea towel, for 30 minutes in a warm place. After that, refrigerate for 4–5 hours or until the dough is firm enough to shape. Ideally, place your dough in the fridge to ferment overnight, which will help develop its flavour.

When ready to bake, roll the dough out to a disc about 1cm/½in thick and 23cm/9in in diameter. Grease and flour a 23cm/9in loose-bottomed cake tin or tart tin. Place your disc in the tin, cover and leave to rise in a warm place for 1–2 hours, or until it has doubled in size.

Meanwhile, make the crumble. Put all the ingredients in a small bowl and rub together with your fingertips until the texture is coarse and sandy. Chill until ready to use.

Make an egg wash by mixing the extra egg yolk and tablespoon of milk together (if you have any egg wash left over from previous bakes, now is the opportunity to use it).

When the brioche has risen, preheat the oven to 200°C/180°C fan/400°F/Gas 6. Brush the egg wash over the top of the dough, sprinkle the crumble over and bake for 15–20 minutes, or until the brioche is a deep golden brown. Leave to cool in the tin.

To make the syrup, bring the water and sugar to a boil in a small saucepan. Remove from the heat, add the vanilla and allow to cool.

When ready to assemble your cake, finish the crème diplomate by whipping the double cream to soft peaks in a large bowl. Whip the cold custard to loosen it up, then fold in the whipped cream in three stages.

Fit a piping bag with a large round nozzle (or improvise by cutting a 1.5cm/⅝in hole at the tip of a disposable piping bag). You could also simply spoon the cream onto the cake and smooth it over with a spatula or tablespoon.

Slice the brioche horizontally in two. Soak each piece with half the syrup, dabbing with a pastry brush until the whole cut surface is soft. Place the bottom section of the brioche on a cake stand or a flat plate. Pipe a ring of water droplet shaped dollops of cream around the edge of the cake. Pipe the remaining cream in the middle in a spiral.

Arrange the peach slices on top of the cream spiral, avoiding damaging your neat scalloped edge. Cover with the crumble-topped layer of brioche and refrigerate until you're ready to enjoy.

Biscuits and
Cookies

Chocolate Anzac biscuits

 25 minutes   10–15 minutes per batch   24 biscuits 1

170g/6oz/¾ cup brown butter (see page 18), made from 240g/8½oz/1 cup plus 1 tbsp unsalted butter

200g/7oz/1½ cups plain (all-purpose) flour

250g/9oz/1¼ cups caster (superfine) sugar

½ tsp salt

140g/5oz/scant 1½ cups rolled oats

110g/3¾oz/1½ cups desiccated (dried shredded) coconut

70g/2½oz/3½ tbsp golden syrup (light corn syrup)

1 tsp bicarbonate of soda (baking soda)

80g/2¾oz/⅓ cup boiling water

200g/7oz dark chocolate (or milk or white chocolate, if you prefer)

½ tsp instant coffee powder (optional)

These iconic biscuits, long associated with the Australian and New Zealand Army Corps established during the First World War, are packed with oat goodness.

It is said that wives sent these to their soldiers abroad because the biscuits kept well, as the ingredients did not spoil easily. They're also affordable and super easy to make.

Anzac biscuits are traditionally made with golden syrup but, with our ethos being that you can bake with what you have available, you can substitute the golden syrup with honey or maple syrup. The biscuits are great plain, but sometimes I like to dip them into chocolate or drizzle them with it.

Make the brown butter according to the instructions on page 18. Strain the butter through a fine-mesh sieve and set aside to cool completely.

Preheat the oven to 180°C/160°C fan/350°F/Gas 4 and line two baking sheets with baking parchment.

In a large bowl, combine the flour, sugar, salt, oats and coconut, mix well, and set aside.

Put the brown butter into a medium saucepan, set over medium heat and stir in the golden syrup. Put the bicarbonate of soda in a cup with the boiling water, mix well, then pour the liquid over the butter mixture and stir – it will immediately become frothy.

Tip the wet ingredients into the dry ingredients and mix until combined.

Using a tablespoon, scoop out portions of the dough and roughly shape them into balls – aim to get 24 evenly sized balls. Put the balls on the prepared baking sheets, taking care to leave at least 5cm/2in between each to allow for spreading. Bake one batch at a time for 10 minutes or, if you like them crunchy, bake for a further 5 minutes. Remove from the oven and transfer to a wire rack to cool.

Once the biscuits have cooled, melt the chocolate with the coffee powder. Dip the lower half of your biscuits into the melted chocolate then sit them back on the rack to set.

The biscuits can be kept in an airtight container for up to 2 weeks, or you can freeze them baked or unbaked (see tip, left).

+ tip

If freezing your biscuits unbaked, don't freeze the whole batch of dough in one lump. Instead, shape the cookies and freeze them on the baking sheet for an hour until the balls have hardened, then transfer them to a freezer bag and freeze. Thaw in the fridge overnight before baking.

Hazelnut chocolate sablé biscuits

 10 minutes + chilling   15 minutes per batch | 24 sandwiches   1

200g/7oz/¾ cup plus 2 tbsp
  salted butter
150g/5½oz/¾ cup caster
  (superfine) sugar
½ tsp salt
2 tsp vanilla extract
2 egg yolks, plus 1 egg yolk for
  the egg wash
300g/10½oz/2¼ cups plain
  (all-purpose) flour (gf plus
  ½ tsp xanthan gum), plus
  extra for dusting
2 tsp milk, for the egg wash
120g/4¼oz/⅓ cup chocolate and
  hazelnut spread, such as Nutella

Sablés Bretons are fine, shiny buttery biscuits that melt-in-the-mouth, but with much more crunch than palets Bretons. They're delicious on their own yet also make irresistible sandwich biscuits when spread with a layer of chocolate. I dare you to make these last more than one day!

In a large bowl, cream together the butter, sugar, salt and vanilla until light and fluffy. Add the egg yolks and mix until well combined. Tip in the flour and use a spatula to mix it all together into a dough – use a hand if needed.

Wrap the dough in some cling film (plastic wrap) or baking parchment, flatten slightly and chill in the fridge for about an hour until the dough firms – if you're in a hurry, put it in the freezer for about 20 minutes.

Preheat the oven to 180°C/160°C fan/350°F/Gas 4 and line a couple of baking sheets with baking parchment.

Lightly flour a work surface and roll out your dough to a sheet 3mm/⅛in thick. Using a 6cm/2½in cookie cutter, cut as many discs as you can from the dough. You should be able to stamp out about 48 rounds.

Mix the egg yolk and milk together in a small dish and brush this over the biscuits. Decorate them with a criss-cross pattern using the back of a fork – gently pressing the tines in one direction and then turning 90 degrees and pressing in the other direction. Or if you have an embossing roller pin, you can use it to add patterns and interest to your biscuits.

Put the biscuits on your baking sheets and bake one batch at a time for 10–15 minutes, or until golden brown. Remove from the oven and allow to cool for a few minutes on the tray before transferring to a wire rack to cool completely.

To assemble, dollop a teaspoon of chocolate hazelnut spread in the middle of the bottom of a biscuit and sandwich together with a second biscuit, pressing gently to push the spread to the edges. Repeat with the remaining biscuits and spread.

The sablés will keep (unfilled) in the cookie jar for up to 2 weeks. The dough can be frozen for up to 6 months. When ready to bake, thaw overnight in the fridge before rolling, cutting and baking as above.

Oatmeal lace cookies

 30 minutes 12 minutes per batch | 24 cookies 1

130g/4½oz/½ cup plus 1 tbsp
   unsalted butter
230g/8oz/1 cup plus 2 tbsp light
   brown soft sugar, or white
   caster (superfine) sugar
180g/6¼oz/scant 2 cups
   rolled oats
20g/⅔oz/2⅓ tbsp plain
   (all-purpose) flour
2 tsp vanilla extract
½ tsp salt
1 large egg (55g/2oz)

Named for their lacy appearance, these thin cookies are crispy on the edge and chewy in the middle. They have a buttery, toffee flavour and are easily made using your last egg, some butter, sugar, flour and oats.

Add citrus zest, chocolate, or a teaspoon of rum, cognac or whisky to vary the taste – you can even throw in a few nuts and dried fruits. Come the festive season, they make great edible gifts that will not break the bank.

Depending on your oven, these cookies will bake within 12 minutes, so you need to keep an eye on them and take them out as soon as the edges are golden brown. The smaller the size of your cookies, the quicker they will bake.

Preheat the oven to 190°C/fan 170°C/375°F/Gas 4 and line two baking sheets with baking parchment or silicone mats.

Put the butter and sugar in a saucepan over a medium heat and stir until they have melted to a thick paste. Remove the pan from the heat and leave to cool a little – if the mixture's too hot, it will scramble the egg when it's added.

Stir in the oats, flour, vanilla, salt and the egg and mix well.

Using a tablespoon, spoon the batter onto the lined baking sheets leaving 5cm/2 inches between the cookies to allow for spreading.

Bake the cookies one batch at a time for 10–12 minutes, or until the edges of the cookies have turned golden brown. Allow your cookies to cool, then remove them from the baking sheet and store in an airtight container, with a sheet of parchment paper between the layers, for up to 1 week, or freeze. You can also freeze the unbaked dough (see tip, page 68).

Cat's tongue biscuits

 20 minutes   8–10 minutes per batch   48 biscuits   1

45g/1½oz/3 tbsp unsalted butter, at room temperature
45g/1½oz/5 tbsp icing (confectioners') sugar
1 tsp vanilla bean paste
a pinch of salt
1 large egg white
45g/1½oz/5 tbsp plain (all-purpose) flour, sifted

Baking often requires the use of egg yolks, leaving you unsure what to do with the egg whites other than make a meringue. I want to maximise the use of all our ingredients, and this is where cat's tongue – *langue de chat* –biscuits and other egg-white-only bakes come to the rescue. Cat's tongues are so easy to put together. There is no need of fancy equipment and a batch takes less than 10 minutes to bake.

Here I am going for vanilla, working with what is commonly found in a pantry, but you could use lemon or orange zest, and dip them in chocolate too, making use of whatever ingredients you have available. The biscuits taste great and are surprisingly addictive bearing in mind that they are made only with flour, egg, sugar, butter and vanilla.

Cat's tongues make a great present around the festive season and are a wonderful accompaniment to desserts such as ice cream. I promise you they won't hang around in the cookie jar for long either.

- -

Preheat the oven to 180°C/160°C fan/350°F/Gas 4 and line two baking sheets with baking parchment or silicone mats.

In a mixing bowl, cream together the butter, icing sugar, vanilla and salt. Add the egg white and mix until combined, then fold in the flour.

Spoon the mixture into a piping bag fitted with a 1cm/½in round nozzle, or cut the end of a disposable piping bag to a similar size. Pipe as many 8cm/3¼in lines as possible onto the lined baking sheets, leaving a 4cm/1½in gap between them to allow the biscuits to spread.

Bake each batch for 8–10 minutes or until the edges are golden brown, but check them regularly after 5 minutes, as ovens do vary.

While the cat's tongues are still warm, transfer them to a wire rack to cool.

Store in an airtight container – they will go soggy if left out in the open too long.

+ tip

If you don't have any piping bags, you could make your own using parchment paper (see pages 12–13). Or you can simply spoon small dollops (about a teaspoon) of the batter onto the baking sheets. I have made round cat's tongues in the past and they were still delicious.

Speculoos biscuits

 20 minutes + chilling   20 minutes per batch   48 biscuits   1

150g/5½oz/¾ cup light brown sugar (or make your own, see page 16)

120g/4¼oz/½ cup salted butter

1 egg

200g/7oz/1½ cups plain (all-purpose) flour, plus extra for dusting

½ tsp baking powder

¼ tsp bicarbonate of soda (baking soda)

1 tsp ground cinnamon

¼ ground nutmeg

¼ ground cloves

¼ ground ginger

a pinch of ground star anise

a pinch of ground cardamom

¼ tsp salt

The flavour of speculoos biscuits evokes the festive season. In fact, they're traditionally baked on St Nicholas Day Eve on the fifth or sixth of December. They're absolutely delicious on their own or with a cup of tea.

The unbaked cookie dough freezes very well, so feel free to make a bigger batch and have a stash ready to bake on demand. It will last in the freezer for up to six months.

- -

In a large bowl, cream the sugar and butter together until light and fluffy. Crack in the egg and mix until well combined. Add the flour, baking powder, bicarbonate of soda, all the spices and the salt and mix to a dough. Wrap the dough in cling film (plastic wrap) or parchment paper, flatten it slightly and place in the fridge until firm. If you are in a hurry, put it in the freezer for about 20 minutes.

Preheat your oven to 180°C/160°C fan/350°F/Gas 4 and line two baking sheets with baking parchment.

Lightly flour a work surface and roll out your dough to a sheet 3mm/⅛in thick. Using a 6cm/2½in cookie cutter (or a small glass), cut as many discs as you can. If you are making this around the festive season and have any festive cookie cutters, use them. If you have an embossing roller pin, you can use it to add patterns and interest to your biscuits too.

Fit as many biscuits as you can onto the prepared trays and transfer to the oven. Bake for 20 minutes, then transfer to a wire rack to cool completely. While they are cooking, keep cutting out biscuits from the remaining dough, re-rolling the offcuts, until you have baked it all.

Your speculoos biscuits will keep in a cookie jar for up to 2 weeks. Like most biscuits, the dough can be frozen for up to 6 months (see tip, page 68). In this case, thaw overnight in the fridge, then follow the steps above.

French meringue macarons

 1 hour 20 minutes | 40 macaron shells 1

140g/5oz/1½ cups finely ground almonds

100g/3½oz/¾ cup icing (confectioner's) sugar

80g/2¾oz egg whites (about 2 egg whites), at room temperature

a pinch of cream of tartar (optional)

food colouring (optional)

100g/3½oz/½ cup caster (superfine) sugar

sesame seeds (optional)

100g/3½oz/scant ½ cup chocolate hazelnut spread, lemon curd or other preserves or spread, to fill

Shop-bought macarons can be expensive, so making your own using leftover egg whites from a previous recipe is a true thrift flex.

There are two methods for making macarons: the Italian meringue method and the French meringue method. In the Italian meringue method, the egg is cooked with a hot syrup that gives the macarons a harder shell and makes them slightly chewier.

For the French meringue method, the egg is whipped directly with the sugar, producing a slightly softer shell and a more delicate crumb. It's also the method that uses the least amount of equipment. French meringue does not require a thermometer to check the sugar temperature or tell you when the syrup might be ready to use. I add some cream of tartar to my egg white to help stabilise the meringue, but you could use a few drops of vinegar, too, if you prefer.

These macarons are plain but, if you want to add food colouring, I recommend powdered or gel food colouring as these introduce minimal liquid to the mix. My favourite filling is lemon curd (see the recipe on page 163 for a quick curd, or use a shop-bought one), but here I have filled them with a hazelnut chocolate spread for ease and convenience. In true thrifty spirit, you could use any preserves you already have at home: other fruit curds, jam, jarred spreads... Go for whichever filling you fancy or have available.

- -

Sift the ground almonds and icing sugar together in a bowl, allowing as much almond through the mesh as you can. You will end up with coarser pieces of ground almond in your sieve; if it's less than 40g/1½oz you do not need to replace it (see tip, left).

Tip the egg white, cream of tartar and food colouring (if using) into a mixing bowl and whip on medium speed using a hand blender or stand mixer until the eggs are frothy.

Add the caster sugar a spoonful at a time, whisking continuously and allowing a few seconds for each batch to dissolve before adding the next. Continue whipping until you have a stiff-peaked meringue.

To fold the almond mixture into the meringue (known in French as *macaronnage* or *macaronage*), sprinkle the almond mixture over the meringue in stages, folding them in between each addition with the intention of removing some of the air from the batter. Keep folding until your batter is at the consistency where it drops slowly and gently like a ribbon when you lift the spatula. Be careful not to over-fold your batter as it will be too loose to pipe. For macarons, an under-folded batter is always better than an over-folded one.

+ thrifty

If you have coarse ground almonds left in your sieve, don't throw them away. Store them in an airtight container and add to any other recipe that calls for ground almonds, such as the French Apple Cake (see page 53), Palets Bretons (see page 82), or Pear Frangipane Tart (see page 106).

I count my folds from the start – about 50–60 folds, sometimes a little more depending on how well you whipped your meringue. As you get closer to that number of folds, start testing your batter for that slow ribbon drop by lifting your spatula every couple of folds. When your batter is ready, pour the mixture into a piping bag fitted with a large round nozzle or improvise by cutting a 1cm/½ inch hole from the end of a disposable piping bag.

Line two baking sheets with baking parchment. (You can pipe one batch at a time if you only have one tray.) Secure the parchment paper to the baking sheet at the edges with some of the batter or a scraping of meringue from the mixing bowl, otherwise the macarons piped at the edges will take on a different shape when the corners of the parchment flap in the circulating air of the oven.

Keeping your piping bag vertical, pipe circles 4cm/1½ in diameter. To ensure a consistent shape, I count '1, 2, 3, lift!' in my head as I pipe each macaron. Leave a 2cm/¾in gap between the circles to allow for spread. Tap your tray vigorously on the work surface to remove any air bubbles, then sprinkle over the sesame seeds. Allow the tray of macarons to sit, at room temperature, so that the surface can dry (this is important for achieving the classic 'feet' on your macarons) – 30 minutes will be enough in most cases, but this depends on the humidity of the room. They are ready to bake when you can touch the macaron shells gently with no batter sticking to your fingers.

While your macaron shells are drying out, preheat the oven at 170°C/160°C fan/ 325°F/Gas 3. When ready to cook, drop the temperature to 160°C/150°C fan/300°F/Gas 2 and bake for 10–15 minutes, or until the macarons no longer wobble and the tops of the shells feel set when gently pressed.

Allow the macarons to cool completely before attempting to remove them from the parchment paper or they will break. If reusing the baking tray for the next batch, gently slide the parchment paper (still holding the macarons) off the tray onto a cooling rack or flat surface.

When your macarons are completely cool, match them in pairs and sandwich them with your chosen filling. Once filled, macarons are at their best when allowed to mature in the fridge for a day.

If you don't want to eat them all, you can freeze them, unfilled, for up to 3 months in an airtight container.

+ tip

Each oven is different and because macarons need so little time and low temperature to bake perfectly, I recommend a few trials to determine whether you want to leave your macarons in a little longer or increase or decrease the temperature of your oven. Either way, your macaron will still turn out delicious and good to fill and enjoy.

Samoa cookies

 2 hours + chilling   **20 minutes per batch**  **24 cookies**

100g/3½oz/7 tbsp butter
70g/2½oz/⅓ cup caster (superfine)
 sugar
¼ tsp salt
1 large egg white (30g/1oz), or
 2 tbsp cold milk
½ tsp vanilla bean paste or vanilla
 extract
180g/6¼oz/1⅓ cups plain
 (all-purpose) flour (gf plus
 ¼ tsp xanthan gum), plus
 extra for dusting

For the topping

150g/5½oz/2 cups desiccated
 (dried shredded) coconut
50g/1¾oz/3½ tbsp water
150g/5½oz/¾ cup caster sugar
30g/1oz/2 tbsp cold unsalted
 butter
100g/3½oz/scant ½ cup double
 (heavy) cream
¼ tsp salt
1 tsp vanilla bean paste or vanilla
 extract
200g/7oz dark chocolate

+ tip

To make beautifully
golden cookies, make
sure the sugar cooks
first to a medium-dark
amber colour before
you add the butter
and cream. Caramel
solidifies once made, so
if you keep it longer on
the stove in an attempt
to reach a dark amber
colour, you'll end up with
hard caramel. Instead,
as soon as the caramel
looks homogenous
remove it from the stove.

The combination of textures – crunchy biscuit base topped with chewy caramel and toasted coconut – adds particular pleasure to eating these. Once baked, they freeze well, so if you have a small household, freeze your batch and take them out as needed.

To make the shortbread, cream together the butter, sugar and salt until light and fluffy. Add the egg white (or milk) and mix until fully combined. Add the vanilla and flour and bring together to a dough. Wrap in cling film (plastic wrap), flatten and chill for 30 minutes.

Meanwhile, line a baking tray with baking parchment or a silicone mat and tip in the desiccated coconut. Preheat the oven to 200°C/ 180°C fan/400°F/Gas 6, adding the tray of coconut to the cold oven so that it toasts for about 10 minutes. Keep an eye on it and when it is light golden, remove from the oven and leave to cool.

To avoid over-working your dough, divide it into three pieces. Lightly flour the work surface and roll the first piece into a 3mm-/⅛in-thick sheet. Using a 6cm/2½in diameter cookie cutter, cut out as many cookies as you can. Using the wide end of a piping nozzle, cut a hole right in the middle of each cookie to form a ring. Remove the excess dough in the centre and set it aside for later.

Line two baking trays with baking parchment or silicone mats to place the cookies on. Repeat the process with the remaining two dough portions, then bring all the excess dough together in a ball. Roll it and cut out more cookies. You should end up with 24 in all. Put 12 cookies on each baking tray and bake both trays at once for 20 minutes until light golden. Set aside to cool.

Meanwhile, put the water for the topping in a small saucepan and add the sugar. Cook to a medium-to-dark amber colour, taking care not to burn the caramel (see tip, left, and page 20). Add the butter and stir until incorporated. Mix in the cream and, when fully combined, remove from the heat and stir in the salt and vanilla. Set aside about 50g/1¾oz of the caramel to use as a glue. Mix the remainder with the toasted coconut and set aside.

Melt your chocolate in a double boiler or microwave. Spread a little of the reserved caramel over each cookie and top with small chunks of the coconut-caramel mixture. Dip the base of the cookies into the melted chocolate, then return them to the baking parchment. Drizzle or pipe the remaining chocolate over the cookies, and allow them to set at room temperature, or in the fridge if in a hurry.

Store the finished cookies in an airtight container for up to 5 days, or freeze for up to 3 months.

Palets Bretons

 10 minutes + chilling   25 minutes | 16 biscuits   1

185g/6½oz/¾ cup butter, at room
  temperature
110g/3¾oz/¾ cup icing
  (confectioners') sugar
2 small egg yolks
160g/5¾oz/scant 1¼ cups plain
  (all-purpose) flour
55g/2oz/½ cup ground almonds
1 tsp vanilla extract
½ tsp salt

Everything from Brittany has to be made with a tonne of butter and these delightful, melt-in-the-mouth biscuits are no exception! They got their name from the board game Le Palet Breton, where players throw cast iron discs onto a wooden board. They make great use of leftover egg yolks, which I often have when I've made an Italian meringue buttercream. You can even use the biscuit dough as a tart base – all you need do is slap on some jam, cream and fresh fruit (see my passionfruit and mango tart on page 108).

If you want to save a few for another time, freeze the biscuits uncooked, then thaw them in the fridge and bake when ready. They do last a good couple of weeks in the biscuit jar, although I doubt they will last that long in reality!

- -

Cream the butter and icing sugar together until light and fluffy. Add the egg yolks, mixing until smooth. Add the flour, almonds, vanilla and salt and mix well until it comes together into a dough.

Tip the mixture onto a sheet of cling film and roll into a log 5cm/2in thick and 23cm/9in long. Chill the log in the fridge until the dough firms up – this will take about an hour, but the freezer is a faster alternative.

Meanwhile, preheat the oven to 180°C/160°C fan/350°F/Gas 4. Use a sharp knife to slice the dough into 16 discs, each 1–1.5cm/ ½–⅝in thick, and pop them into muffin moulds (see tip). Bake for 25 minutes or until golden brown. Leave to cool in the muffin moulds for a few minutes, then turn the biscuits out onto a wire rack to cool completely.

Your biscuits will keep in a cookie jar for up to 2 weeks, or the dough can be frozen for up to 6 months (see tip, page 68).

+ tip

I use two eight-hole silicone muffin moulds to make these, as their straight sides mean the biscuits don't have sloped edges and look more traditional. However, you can use whatever you have – it won't affect the flavour of the biscuit.

Brown butter chocolate chip cookies

 20 minutes + chilling   12 minutes per batch   12 cookies   1

110g/3¾oz/½ cup brown butter (see page 18) made from 150g/5½oz/⅔ cup unsalted butter

75g/2½oz/6 tbsp caster (superfine) sugar

125g/4½oz/⅔ cup less 2 tsp soft light brown sugar

1 large egg (55g/2oz)

1 tsp vanilla extract

150g/5½oz/1 cup plus 2 tbsp plain (all-purpose) flour (gf plus ¼ tsp xanthan gum)

½ tsp bicarbonate of soda (baking soda)

½ tsp salt

50g/1¾oz dark (bittersweet) chocolate of your choice, chopped

100g/3½oz milk chocolate, chopped

sea salt flakes or coarse salt, to sprinkle (optional)

What is better than a chocolate chip cookie? Crunchy on the edges, soft and chewy in the middle. But, hold on a minute because we are not going to use chocolate chips to make these. Chocolate chips have added stabilisers that prevent them from properly melting – that's not great when we want a gooey cookie. Instead, we are going to use a simple chocolate bar to get that melting, oozing chocolate texture that comes with warm, freshly baked cookies.

What is better is that 100g/3½oz of supermarket brand chocolate will cost you three times less than a 100g/3½oz bag of chocolate chips. What is there not to like? I always have a few half-opened chocolate bars in my pantry and you can make these cookies using any leftover chocolate from other bakes in this book. You can even try using different flavoured chocolates, such as orange or hazelnut.

Make the brown butter according to the instructions on page 18. Strain the butter through a fine-mesh sieve and place in the freezer for 20 minutes to cool completely.

Put the cooled brown butter in a medium bowl, add both sugars and mix until well combined. Add the egg and vanilla and mix again until incorporated. Sift in the flour and bicarbonate of soda, add the salt and mix thoroughly, but not too much – overmixing will introduce air to your batter and result in a cakey cookie rather than a chewy one. Fold in the chopped chocolates, then refrigerate the dough for 30 minutes, or overnight for a deeper flavour.

Meanwhile, preheat your oven to 200°C/180°C fan/400°F/Gas 6 and line two baking sheets with baking parchment or silicone mats.

Scoop out 12 balls of dough (about a tablespoon each) and arrange on the baking sheets, allowing 5cm/2in between the cookies for spread. (You can choose to freeze some of the dough at this point – see tip, pâtissière 68 – or bake it all.) Sprinkle the top of the cookies with sea salt flakes.

Bake the cookies one tray at a time for 8–12 minutes, so that the edges look set but the centres are still doughy. Timing will depend on how chewy or crunchy you want them, with 10 minutes being a bit of both. Remove the cookies from the oven and allow them to set on the tray for a few minutes before transferring to a wire rack to cool, although they are extra delicious enjoyed warm.

The cookies will keep in a cookie jar for up to 2 weeks.

+ thrifty

Remember, too, that you can also make your own brown or golden caster sugar way cheaper than shop bought packs – check out the method on page 16.

Palmiers

 30 minutes + chilling   25 minutes per batch 🍴 12 palmiers

For the beurre manié

250g/9oz/1 cup plus 2 tbsp unsalted butter (minimum 82% fat), softened, plus extra for greasing

100g/3½oz/¾ cup strong white bread flour

For the dough

180g/6¼oz/1 ⅓ cups strong white bread flour, plus extra for dusting

100g/3½oz/7 tbsp water

½ tsp white vinegar

2.5g/¹⁄₁₆oz/½ rounded tsp salt

120g/4¼oz/½ cup plus 2 tbsp caster (superfine) sugar, plus extra for dusting

For the egg wash

1 egg yolk

1 tsp milk

Palmiers are at the top of our favourite biscuit list and every time we pass through Gare du Nord in Paris on our way to see friends and family we buy some. Crunchy buttery, and caramelly, they melt in your mouth and are simply a joy to eat. I love pulling out the little flaky bits and savouring them slowly.

If you're in a hurry, you could use shop-bought puff pastry, but really I want you to make your own. Not only will it be made from pure butter, we'll be using a recipe for inverted puff pastry which gives your biscuits more crunch and – a bit like rough puff – is more forgiving than normal puff pastry.

The first step to inverted puff pastry is making a beurre manié, which is simply a butter paste made by working room-temperature butter together with some flour and then chilling it.

- -

To make the beurre manié, beat the butter and flour together, either by hand using a spatula, or in a stand mixer with the mixing attachment. The resulting paste should be creamy. Tip the beurre manié onto some baking parchment and fold it into a square shape. Roll over it with a rolling pin until you have a neat square slab roughly 1.5cm/⅝in thick and place in the fridge to set.

To make the dough, put all the ingredients except the sugar in a stand mixer and mix until you have a smooth homogenous dough. Alternatively, if making by hand, put the flour in a mixing bowl and create a well in the centre. Add all the other ingredients except the sugar and mix to a dough.

Shape the dough into a square the same size as your slab of beurre manié and place in the fridge to set. If you're in a hurry, freeze for about 20 minutes. You want both doughs to be of the same consistency.

Once the beurre manié and dough have set, lightly flour your work surface with some bread flour. Stack the beurre manié under the dough and roll them out together into a rectangular strip about 50cm/20in long and 5mm/¼in thick. When you fold, the butter should be outside and the dough inside.

Now you're going to do a 'double turn'. Bring both short ends of the dough into the middle of the strip, so that they touch but do not overlap. Fold again in half like a book, so you have four layers. Wrap the dough in cling film (plastic wrap) and leave to rest in the fridge for 30 minutes.

Making sure the opening of your dough book is on your right-hand side, repeat the above rolling and folding step (that will be your second 'double turn'). Use your rolling pin to flatten the dough a little, wrap again in cling film and leave to rest for another 30 minutes in the fridge.

For your final 'single turn', sprinkle the dough with the sugar and, again with the opening on the right side, roll it into a strip 50cm/20in long. This time, fold it up to give three layers, not four. Your pastry is now ready.

To shape the biscuits, roll out the pastry to a sheet measuring about 70 x 20cm/28 x 8in, and 5mm/⅝in thick. Fold both short edges in to meet in the middle. Now do the same movement again, bringing the folded edges to the middle, a bit like a butterfly. Using your rolling pin, press down on the middle of the pastry and fold in half again, like closing a book, so that you have a flat log with eight layers.

Preheat the oven to 220°C/200°C fan/425°F/Gas 7. Generously butter two baking sheets and dust them generously with sugar.

Slice the pastry log into 12-or-so slices 1cm/½in thick. Place six palmiers on each sheet, leaving space around each one for them to expand. In a small dish, whisk the egg yolk and milk together to make an egg wash, then brush this lightly over the biscuits. Bake one tray at a time (leaving the other in the fridge while you bake the first) for 20–25 minutes until puffed up and a lovely caramel colour. Transfer your biscuits to a wire rack to cool.

The palmiers will keep in an airtight container for a couple of days, or you can freeze them in an airtight freezer bag for up to 3 months. If frozen, they will need to go back in the oven for about 15 minutes to crisp up again. If you want to freeze the pastry uncooked, do this *before* the last single turn and without adding any sugar. When you want to bake, you can thaw your pastry, then do the last single turn (sprinkling it with the sugar) and bake as above.

Pastries
and Tarts

Spinach and mushroom quiche

 40 minutes + chilling   25 minutes   8   2

For the shortcrust pastry

210g/7½oz/1½ cups plain (all-purpose) flour (gf plus 1 tsp xanthan gum), plus extra for dusting
130g/4½oz/½ cup plus 1 tbsp cold butter
1 large egg (55g)
1 tbsp cold water
¼ tsp salt

For the custard

15g/½oz/1 tbsp butter
leaves from 3 thyme sprigs
1 small yellow onion (about 50g/1¾oz), finely chopped
2 eggs
120g/4¼oz/½ cup double (heavy) cream
1 chicken or vegetable stock cube, crumbled
1 tsp Dijon mustard
¼ tsp salt
pinch of black pepper

For the filling

30g/1oz/2 tbsp butter
250g/9oz mushrooms, sliced
½ tsp garlic powder
a pinch of salt
250g/9oz baby spinach leaves
80g/2¾oz grated Gruyère cheese

+ thrifty

Frozen spinach is much cheaper in weight than fresh spinach, so feel free to use it here. If you do, allow it to thaw and drain first.

It's often said that quiche is old fashioned, but there is nothing old fashioned about this one. It's a crumbly, super-short, melt-in-your-mouth pastry filled with buttery spinach and creamy custard.

Gruyère is the perfect cheese for quiche and a little goes a long way, but if it's not available, you can substitute with Emmental, Comté, Jarlsberg or Beaufort. Cheddar is an option, too, and you will get a delicious quiche using it, but with a very different flavour.

- -

To make the shortcrust pastry, in a large bowl rub the flour and butter together with your fingertips until sandy in texture. (You can use a food processor to speed up this process.) Add the egg, water and salt and bring together into a dough without overworking it. Wrap in cling film (plastic wrap) and chill in the fridge – you always want to work with cold pastry as it's much easier to handle.

When ready, lightly flour a work surface and roll out the dough to a circle about 30cm in diameter and 3mm/⅛in thick. Use your rolling pin to lift it up and lay it over a 23cm/9in tart tin, so there is an overhang of pastry at the top. Using a straight-sided glass, ease the pastry into the corners of the tin by rolling the glass around the edge in circular motion. Chill for 20 minutes.

Preheat your oven at 200°C/180°C fan/400°F/Gas 6. Line your chilled pastry case with parchment paper, fill it with baking beans or cheap pulses (see equipment section) and blind bake for 15 minutes. Lift out the baking beans and parchment paper and continue baking for a further 10 minutes to dry out the base.

Meanwhile, make the custard. Put the butter, thyme and onion in a small frying pan over medium heat and cook until the onion is soft and transparent. Set aside to cool slightly. In a medium bowl, whisk together the eggs, cream, stock cube, mustard, salt and pepper, adding the cooked onions. Set aside.

Prepare the filling using the same pan you used to cook the onions. Heat the butter, add the mushrooms, garlic and salt, and cook over high heat until the mushrooms are soft and most of the water has evaporated. Add the spinach and cook until it has wilted and the mixture is thick.

Tip the spinach mixture into the prebaked tart case and spread it around evenly. Sprinkle over the grated cheese, then pour in the custard, making sure it's distributed evenly. Bake at 200°C/180°C fan/400°F/Gas 6 for 20–25 minutes, or until the middle of the quiche looks set and the top is slightly golden. Enjoy warm.

Steak and kidney bean pie

 1 hour – 1 hour 20 minutes + chilling 40 minutes  6 3

butter, for greasing

1 recipe quantity inverted puff pastry (omitting the sugar, see page 86), a 500g/1lb 2oz block of ready-made all-butter puff pastry, or 2 sheets of ready-rolled puff pastry (gf)

1 egg yolk

1 tsp milk

For the filling

1½ tsp garlic powder

1 tsp ground ginger

½ tsp black pepper

a pinch of cayenne pepper

1 tsp salt

1 beef stock cube (or use any flavour you have) (gf)

3 tbsp cooking oil

500g/1lb 2oz braising steak, cut into 1.5cm/⅝in pieces

2 tbsp cornflour (cornstarch)

200g/7oz diced onion

leaves from 2 thyme sprigs

1 bay leaf

200g/7oz peeled and diced carrot

1 stalk celery, finely diced

100g/3½oz diced red (bell) peppers

2 x 400g/14oz cans kidney beans, drained and rinsed (gf)

100g/3½oz/scant ½ cup water

1 tsp soy sauce or Worcestershire sauce (gf)

sea salt and black pepper

+ thrifty

I use canned beans, not only for speed but to save on energy, because pulses take a long time to cook without a pressure cooker.

I always like to make my own pastry, but you could opt for shop-bought – in which case a block of puff pastry will be much cheaper than ready-rolled, and frozen pastry is cheaper than chilled. How you choose to line the dish will determine how much pastry you need, too. Because I love puff pastry, I line the bottom and top of the pie, but if you prefer, you can just line the top, which means you'll only need half as much. Use any scraps to decorate your pie.

Use whatever vegetables you have available and also feel free to swap the beef for sausages, lamb or chicken, if that's what you have. I'm using braising steak and I dice it myself because doing your own food prep is always lighter on the pocket.

- -

Start by making the filling. In a small dish, mix together the spices, salt, stock cube, and 1 tablespoon of the cooking oil to make a rub. Add half the rub to the diced beef and mix well. Sprinkle with the cornflour and stir to coat the meat. Heat 1 tablespoon of cooking oil in a large frying pan, then tip in the beef and fry over medium heat, stirring occasionally, until the meat has browned. Remove from the frying pan and set aside.

Add the last tablespoon of oil to the pan. Add the onion, thyme, bay and the remaining rub and cook on low until the onion is brown and begins to caramelise. Add the carrot, celery and peppers and cook for a further 5 minutes.

Add the beans, water, soy or Worcestershire sauce and cooked beef to the pan and simmer for 5 minutes. Use the back of a wooden spoon to mash about one-third of the beans to thicken the stew. Leave to simmer and reduce for another 10 minutes, then taste and, if it needs it, season with salt. Remove the pan from the heat and let the pie filling cool completely.

Preheat the oven to 220°C/200°C fan/425°F/Gas 7. Grease a 28 x 23cm/11¼ x 9in rectangular pie dish with butter or choose a similar-sized ovenproof dish big enough to contain your bean stew.

Divide your pastry into two pieces. Roll the first piece into a 2mm-/ ¹⁄₁₆in-thick sheet, long and wide enough to line the base and sides of your dish. Transfer the pastry to the dish, using the rolling pin to help you, and pour in the cold stew. Roll out the pastry for the top so that it's large enough to cover the top of your pie. Lay it over the filling, trim the edges and crimp with the bottom layer of pastry to seal. Use any pastry scraps to decorate the top of your pie.

Mix the egg yolk with the milk and brush it over the pastry. Bake for 35–40 minutes, or until the pastry is risen and golden brown.

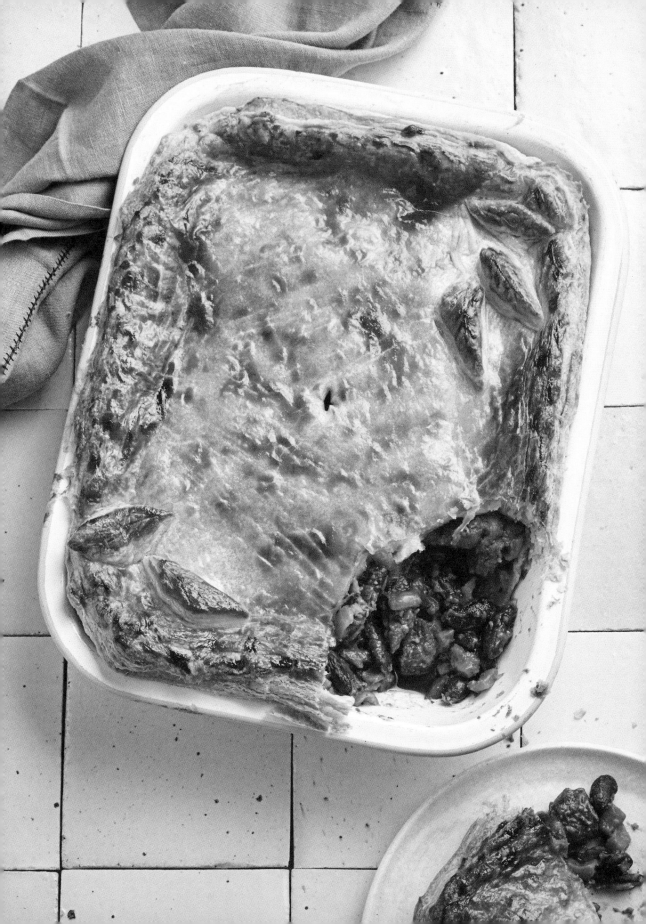

Minced beef pastels

 20 minutes 20 minutes 12–14   1

For the pastry
300g/10½oz/2¼ cups plain
  (all-purpose) flour, plus extra
  for dusting
5g/⅛in/1 tsp salt
30g/1oz/2 tbsp butter, oil, beef
  shortening or lard at room
  temperature
1 large egg
50g/1¾oz/3½ tbsp warm water
1 tsp white vinegar (optional, see
  tip below)
about 500g/17oz/2 cups
  vegetable oil, for deep-frying

For the beef filling
2 tbsp vegetable oil or butter
1 small–medium onion, finely
  chopped
1 garlic clove, finely chopped
leaves from 1 thyme sprig,
  or a bay leaf (optional)
1 medium carrot, peeled and
  finely chopped
½ sweet (bell) pepper, diced (any
  colour, or substitute any frozen
  veg you like)
1 tbsp finely chopped parsley
½ tsp ground ginger
½ tsp black pepper
¼ tsp cayenne pepper
1 vegetable stock cube or stock pot
½ tsp salt, or to taste
250g/9oz minced (ground) beef

+ tip
The vinegar in the dough
is optional but it affects
the gluten development
of the flour and therefore
helps your dough stay
tender.

I am often asked to produce bakes from Benin, where I was born. Thanks to its coastal position, the country has a history of foreign influences. When growing up ovens were not a standard kitchen appliance, so most of our local bakes, like pastels, were deep fried.

Popular in Brazil, where they're known as empanadas, these filled pastries somehow found their way to Benin. They are a great way to use up leftovers; try leftover chicken, pork or fish brought together with those last few carrots, the onion lurking in the fridge, a stock cube, and a few herbs and spices like parsley, oregano, black pepper, cayenne, ginger, and garlic, and you're away!

First, make the dough. In a bowl, combine the flour, salt and fat and rub them between your fingers until sandy. Add the egg, warm water and vinegar, if using. Knead briefly, just until your dough is smooth, then shape it into a ball. Place in a bowl, cover with a towel and allow to rest.

Meanwhile, make the filling. Heat the oil or butter in a pan and add the onion, garlic and thyme. Cook for several minutes until the onion softens. Add the carrot, pepper, parsley, spices, vegetable stock and salt. Cook, stirring, for about 2 minutes. Add the beef and continue cooking until the meat is well browned, then set aside to cool.

To assemble your pastels, divide your dough into 12 equal portions and shape them into balls. On a flour-dusted surface, roll out each ball to give a 10cm/4in disc – the finer you roll your pastry, the crispier your pastel will be. Just how I like them!

Place a tablespoon of your beef filling in the centre of each disc, leaving space around the edges to close the pastry. Fold one half of the pastry over to enclose the filling and form a semi-circular shape. Press the edges firmly together with a fork to seal. Repeat to make 12 pastries.

In a medium, heavy-based saucepan, heat the oil for deep-frying. Test whether it's hot enough to start cooking by adding some of the dough scrapings to the oil – when they sizzle and turn golden brown, the oil is ready.

Once the oil is hot, cook your pastels, three at a time, for about 3 minutes, or until golden brown. Remove them from the oil with a slotted spoon and sit them on paper towels to absorb any excess oil, then pop them on plates and enjoy while still warm.

These go soggy if stored in the fridge, so if you don't need them all, it's best to freeze them (uncooked) and cook when required.

Herby chicken and leek pies

 1 hour + chilling 40 minutes 6 3

For the rough puff pastry

180g/6¼oz/1⅓ cups plain (all-purpose) flour, plus extra for dusting

50g/1¾oz/3½ tbsp beef dripping, at room temperature

½ tsp salt

100g/3½oz/½ cup less 1 tbsp cold unsalted butter, cut in 1cm/½in cubes

100g/3½oz/7 tbsp ice-cold water

½ tsp white vinegar

1 egg, beaten with 1 tbsp milk, for egg-washing

(400g/14oz gf ready-made puff pastry)

For the filling

50g/1¾oz/3½ tbsp butter

500g/1lb 2oz leeks, sliced thickly

250g/9oz carrots, roughly chopped

leaves from 2 thyme sprigs

1 bay leaf

1 stock cube (gf)

2 tsp garlic powder

½ tsp black pepper

3 tbsp Dijon mustard (gf)

2 cooked chicken breasts, shredded

250g/9oz double (heavy) cream

1 tsp salt, or to taste

2 tbsp parsley, finely chopped

+ thrifty

It works out much cheaper to buy a whole chicken than just the breasts. I got the whole chicken and roasted it; I used the two legs for dinner, removed the breasts for these pies and made a delicious soup with the rest!

These pies are the bomb! And what makes them so special is the beef dripping. You thought it was going to be something expensive, right? Beef dripping is cheaper than butter yet packs pastry with flavour and makes it crumbly, too. Make one large pie, if you prefer.

- -

To make the pastry, combine the flour and beef dripping in a large bowl and rub them together to give a sandy texture. (A food processor will speed up this process.) Add the salt, cold butter, water and vinegar. Mix everything by hand so that it comes together as a dough, but you can still see the pieces of butter in it. Wrap the dough in some cling film (plastic wrap), flatten it to create a rough square shape, and place in the fridge to rest for 20 minutes.

On a floured work surface, roll the dough into a rectangle roughly 10cm/4in wide and 45cm/18in long. Fold the two short ends in so that they meet at the centre, to create two layers. Fold one side of the folded dough over onto the other side of the folded dough like a book. You now have four layers and what is called a 'double turn'.

Turn the dough 90 degrees so that the short end faces you and the flaps are on your right, like a closed book. Roll out the dough in the same way and do a second double turn. Refrigerate for 30 minutes.

With the short end facing you again, roll the dough out into another 10 x 45cm/4 x 18in rectangle, but this time fold it in three, like a letter, folding the bottom third up and the top third down over it – this is a single turn. Repeat the single turn so that you have now done two double and two single turns. Wrap the dough in cling film and set aside until ready to use.

To make the filling, place a large saucepan over medium-high heat. Add the butter, leeks, carrots, thyme and bay leaf, and crumble in the stock cube. Cook for about 5 minutes until the vegetables have softened. Add the garlic, black pepper and mustard, mix well and cook for another 2 minutes. Add the shredded chicken and cream, mix well, then season with the salt. Leave to simmer for 5 minutes, then stir in the parsley and allow the filling to cool completely.

Preheat the oven to 190°C/180°C fan/375°F/Gas 5. Roll out your pastry to fit the tops of six small pie dishes. Divide the cooled filling between the dishes and lay the pastry sheets over the top. Crimp the edges of each pie by pinching the dough all the way around the tin. Score the top of the pastry with a small, sharp knife, then brush all over with the egg wash. Bake for 40 minutes until the pastry is golden and risen and the filling is piping hot.

Potato and beef curry pie

 30 minutes 25 minutes | 8 3

1 x 250g/9oz pack filo (phyllo)
    pastry
100g/3½oz/scant ½ cup butter
50g/1¾oz/3½ tbsp vegetable oil
    or olive oil

For the filling

2 tsp vegetable oil
½ tsp ground cumin
3 green cardamom pods, crushed
1 bay leaf
leaves from 2 thyme sprigs
4 large garlic cloves, finely
    chopped
250g/9oz onions, finely chopped
2 tsp curry powder
1 tsp ground ginger
½ tsp garam masala
½ tsp ground black pepper
200g/7oz fresh tomatoes (about
    3 medium vine tomatoes),
    chopped
250g/9oz minced (ground) beef
400g/14oz potatoes, peeled and
    cubed
50g/1¾oz/3½ tbsp water
1 beef stock cube
½ tsp salt, or to taste
a little chilli powder, cayenne or
    other spicy pepper, to taste
300g/10½oz frozen petit pois

+ tip

With a dish like this, I
always do all the veg
prep before I start
cooking to make the
process a breeze.

When you are on a budget, using minced meat – be it beef,
chicken, turkey or pork – can be a great way to stretch your protein
and make something hearty for the whole family out of a couple of
hundred grams of meat. Bulk it up with frozen or fresh vegetables,
add herbs and spices and a sauce of some sort (cream, mustard,
tomato...), and you'll have something delicious that can work with
pasta, rice or, in our case, inside a pie.

Here, I'm adding a few wrinkly potatoes and some peas from
the freezer – you could use cauliflower, carrots, sweet potatoes,
frozen corn or any similar vegetable you fancy.

To make the filling, heat the 2 teaspoons oil in a heavy-based pan,
add the cumin, cardamom, bay leaf and thyme, and cook for a
minute or so to release their flavours. Add the garlic and onions and
cook for about 5 minutes until the onion is translucent. Add the curry
powder, ginger, garam masala, black pepper and tomatoes and
cook until the tomatoes start to look mushy. Add the minced beef
and cook, breaking the meat up with a spatula, until browned.

Add the potatoes and water, crumble in the stock cube, and simmer
for 10 minutes or until the potatoes are soft but not mushy and the
liquid has almost evaporated. Add the salt and chilli powder (or
other fiery spice) to taste. Stir in the peas and set aside (don't worry
about them cooking as they'll do so in the oven).

Preheat the oven to 200°C/180°C fan/400°F/Gas 6 and lightly
grease a 25cm/10in pie dish (you could also use an ovenproof skillet
or shallow casserole).

Unpack the filo pastry. Melt the butter and stir in the oil, then, using
a pastry brush, brush a generous amount of this mixture over
the first sheet of filo. Use it to line half the bottom of your pie dish,
leaving the ends slightly overhanging the rim of the dish. Repeat
with the next sheet, this time laying it over the other half of the pie
dish, so that the whole base is now covered. Or if the sheets are
large, you may be able to cover the whole dish with one.

Turn the pie dish 45 degrees and repeat this buttering and layering
process until you have used half the pack of filo. Pour in the meat
filling and spread level. Working with one sheet at a time, butter
each of the remaining sheets of filo and scrunch them up. Cover the
top of the pie with the scrunched-up filo and tuck in the edges so
it all looks tidy. Brush over any remaining butter mixture and bake
for 25 minutes or until the pastry is golden brown. Enjoy warm on its
own, with more vegetables, or with a salad.

Galette des Rois (King Cake)

 30–50 minutes + chilling 40 minutes 8 2

1 recipe quantity inverted puff pastry (see page 86 and method below), a 500g/1lb 2oz block of ready-made all-butter puff pastry, or 2 sheets of ready-rolled puff pastry *(gf)*

75g/2½oz/⅓ cup butter, at room temperature

75g/2½oz/½ cup plus ½ tbsp icing (confectioners') sugar

1 tsp vanilla extract

¼ tsp salt

2 tsp rum or brandy, or 1 tsp almond extract or orange flower water (optional)

1 large egg, plus 1 yolk for the egg wash

15g/½oz/1 tbsp double (heavy) cream (optional)

75g/2½oz/¾ cup ground almonds

15g/½oz/1½ tbsp instant custard powder (or substitute with cornflour (cornstarch)

1 tsp milk, for egg wash

+ tip

You could use the left-over egg white from the glaze to whip up a batch of cat's tongue biscuits (see page 73) at the same time.

Galette des Rois is a French pie made of frangipane sandwiched between two layers of flaky puff pastry. It's a cake made on Epiphany Day (January 6) and symbolises the arrival of the Three Wise Men in Bethlehem. Traditionally, a fève (originally a bean, but later replaced by a small porcelain figurine) is placed inside the galette. Whoever finds the fève becomes king for the day.

Depending on whether you buy the pastry or make it yourself, this recipe can be dead easy or a little ambitious. If you do choose to buy, make sure it is an all-butter puff pastry. I often make my own, as it is cheaper and homemade is always my preference. Here I'm using the same inverted puff pastry recipe I use to make palmiers (see page 86) but omit the sugar in the final turn.

For simplicity, I skip the usual crème pâtissière in the filling and instead replace it with a few drops of double cream and some instant custard powder. If you have any, great; if not, think of it as optional.

Rum or almond extract is added to give the frangipane extra flavour, but you can omit this if you prefer. If you really don't like almonds, you could make a chocolate, crème pâtissière or even a fruit-filled version of this cake.

If you're making your own pastry, follow the inverted puff pastry from my palmiers recipe on page 86, but do the final and single turn without adding the sugar.

Roll your pastry into a 25 x 50cm/10 x 20in rectangle about 3mm/⅛in thick (unless using ready-rolled pastry). Cut it in half so you have two squares. Skip this step if you're using ready-rolled.

Using a sharp knife and a 23cm/9in cake tin, plate, or pastry ring as a template, cut a disc from each pastry square. Transfer each disc to a baking tray, cover with baking parchment or cling film (plastic wrap) and place in the fridge to chill while you make the filling.

In a medium bowl, cream together the butter, icing sugar, vanilla and salt – plus the alcohol or other flavouring, if using – until light and fluffy. Add the whole egg and mix until well combined, then stir in the cream, if using. Add the ground almonds and custard powder and mix to a paste. If you find your mixture's a little runny, chill it for 30 minutes so that the butter firms up.

+ thrifty

In the past, when making my own was not an option, I've used one sheet of ready-rolled puff pastry, spread half with my frangipane cream and folded the other half on top like a book. It doesn't give the traditional galette shape but you end up using less pastry and have no scraps – something to bear in mind if you are after convenience and simplicity, and want to save money at the same time.

If you are left with pastry scraps, you can save them and use them to top a pie. It will look very rustic but nonetheless will taste amazing. See pages 17 and 106 for other tips for using up leftover pastry.

Prepare an egg wash by mixing the extra egg yolk with the 1 teaspoon of milk.

When you're ready to assemble the galette, pipe or spread the almond cream on top of one of the discs, leaving a 2cm/¾in rim around the edge bare. If adding a fève bean or figurine, now is the time to do it. Brush some egg wash around the rim of the pastry, then top with the second pastry disc and press to seal around the edge.

Scallop the rim of the galette by pressing your index finger on the edge of the pastry and, right next to it, use the back of a small, pointed knife to draw the pastry in. Move your finger right of the knife mark and repeat until you have crimped all the way around the pastry. Brush the top of the galette with some egg wash, avoiding the crimped edge, and place in the fridge for 20 minutes. Meanwhile, preheat your oven to 220°C/200°C fan/425°F/Gas 7.

Remove your galette from the fridge and brush the top again with the remaining egg wash. Use the knife or a scoring blade to score the top of your galette with lines in any desired pattern – let yourself to be creative here.

Bake for 20 minutes, then lower the temperature to 200°C/180°C fan/400°F/Gas 6 and continue baking for another 20 minutes or until golden brown. Enjoy warm.

White chocolate and raspberry curd tart

 1 hour 20 minutes + chilling 25 minutes  8 3

For the pastry

230g/8oz/1¾ cups plain (all-purpose) flour *(gf plus 1 tsp xanthan gum)*, plus extra for dusting

20g/⅔oz/2½ tbsp unsweetened cocoa powder

150g/5½oz/⅔ cup unsalted butter, softened

120g/4¼oz/¾ cup plus 2 tbsp icing (confectioners') sugar

¼ tsp salt

1 large egg

1 tsp vanilla bean paste or vanilla extract

30g/1oz/⅓ cup ground almonds

For the raspberry curd

400g/14oz frozen or fresh raspberries, plus a few fresh ones for decoration

150g/5½oz/¾ cup caster (superfine) sugar

50g/1¾oz/3½ tbsp lemon juice

4 egg yolks

15g/½oz/2 tbsp cornflour (cornstarch)

1 tsp finely grated lemon zest

150g/5½oz/⅔ cup butter, cubed

For the ganache

300g/10½oz white chocolate, chips or chopped

100g/3½oz/scant ½ cup double (heavy) cream

1 tsp vanilla bean paste or vanilla extract

Chocolate pairs beautifully with raspberries and here the sweetness of white chocolate ganache cuts through the tartness of the fruit and really brings this dessert together.

Don't hesitate to use frozen berries. Fresh raspberries are more than double the price of frozen and, when out of season, can look rather pale. In general, frozen berries are great for curds, jams and coulis and, according to research, they hold more nutritional value than fresh ones. They cook much quicker too and, because they are fully ripe when picked, they have a more intense colour that will add vibrancy to your bake.

Planning and preparing bakes in advance can make the process light work and enjoyable. To get up to two days ahead on this one, make your curd and keep it in the fridge, and bake your pastry case and store it an airtight container.

- -

To make the pastry, sift the flour and cocoa together and set aside.

In a separate bowl, cream together the butter and icing sugar until smooth and fluffy. Add the salt, egg and vanilla and mix until fully incorporated. Stir in the ground almonds, then mix in the flour and cocoa mixture until it just comes together (overmixing will make your pastry tough). Wrap the dough in cling film (plastic wrap), flatten it into a disc and chill until firm – about 2 hours in the fridge or 30 minutes in the freezer.

When ready, lightly flour the work surface and roll out the dough to a circle 30cm/12in diameter and 3mm/⅛in thick. Use your rolling pin to help lift and lay it over a 23cm/9in tart tin, so there is an overhang of pastry at the sides. Using a straight-edged glass, ease the pastry into the corners of the tin by rolling the glass around the side. Chill for 20 minutes. Once the pastry has firmed up, use a round-bladed knife to trim the edges so that they're neat.

Meanwhile, preheat your oven to 200°C/180°C fan/400°F/Gas 6. Line the pastry case with parchment paper and fill with ceramic baking beans or cheap pulses (see page 11) and blind bake for 15 minutes. Remove the beans and paper and cook for another 10 minutes, then leave to cool completely before taking it out of the tin.

To make the raspberry curd, put the raspberries, sugar and lemon juice in a medium saucepan. Bring to a simmer and cook until the raspberries are soft and mushy.

Sit a fine-meshed sieve over a bowl, pour the cooked raspberries into it and use a spatula to help separate the seeds from the pulp.

Scrape any pulp that clings under the sieve into the bowl as we are not wasting a thing! Discard the seeds in the sieve.

In a separate bowl, whisk the egg yolks, cornflour and lemon zest together until smooth. Temper the eggs by adding the hot raspberry juice in a slow, steady stream, whisking continuously until fully incorporated. Return the mixture to the saucepan and place over a low heat. Stir continuously with a spatula until the mixture has thickened.

Remove the pan from the heat and whisk in the butter until fully incorporated. Pour the curd into a bowl, cover the surface with cling film and allow to cool, then chill for 30 minutes to cool further.

To make the ganache, put the chocolate and cream in a microwavable bowl and microwave in 30-second intervals, stirring well in between, until the chocolate has fully melted. Allow to cool, then chill for 30 minutes or until completely cool and set but don't let it set hard or you may struggle to whip it. When ready, your ganache should have a thick, spreadable consistency.

Using an electric hand whisk, whip the ganache until light and fluffy, then add the vanilla and mix until fully incorporated. Transfer to a piping bag fitted with a St-Honoré nozzle (see page 13 for how to improvise) or any nozzle of your choice. Set aside until ready to use.

To assemble the tart, put the tart case on a cake stand or flat plate. Remove the curd from the fridge and stir just a little to loosen it up. Pour the curd into the tart case and smooth the surface with a spatula. Pipe the white chocolate ganache around the edges in a zig-zag motion. Decorate with a few fresh raspberries for colour and some lemon zest if you have any left. Place in the fridge until ready to eat and enjoy chilled.

Pear frangipane tart

 25 minutes + chilling 40 minutes | 8 2

For the sweet shortcrust pastry
180g/6¼oz/¾ cup unsalted butter
100g/3½oz/¾ cup icing (confectioners') sugar
5g/⅛oz/1 tsp salt
1 large egg
45g/1½oz/½ cup ground almonds
1 tsp vanilla bean paste or vanilla extract
300g/10½oz/2¼ cups strong white bread flour (gf), plus extra for dusting

For the frangipane
125g/4½oz/½ cup) butter, at room temperature
125g/4½oz/¾ cup plus 2 tbsp icing (confectioners') sugar
2 large eggs
125g/4½oz/1¼ cups ground almonds
1 tsp vanilla bean paste or extract
1 tbsp brandy or rum (optional)
20g/⅔oz/scant ¼ cup cornflour (cornstarch)

For the pear topping
3 pears
1 tbsp butter, melted
1 tbsp sugar

+ thrity
If you're left with any shortcrust pastry scraps, you can make biscuits that you can top with jam or spread and enjoy with a cup of tea. See pages 17 and 102 for other tips for using up leftover pastry.

When I buy pears, once they have spent a few days in the fruit bowl they start to look bruised and uninviting. The longer they spend in that bowl, the less appealing they become! I find fruit tarts are a great way to use them up.

There is always the option to buy ready-made shortcrust pastry; if you do, look in the frozen section because that will be cheaper than the fresh chiller aisle. That said, even if I was after convenience, shortcrust pastry is one dough I would never get from the shop. This is because it's one of the simplest pastries to make and homemade is so much cheaper than the shop-bought version. You can have shortcrust pastry made and resting in the fridge in less than ten minutes.

This tart can be baked, then frozen and reheated another day. It uses similar ingredients to the apple cake on page 53, so I suggest baking them at or around the same time, to make full use of your ingredients.

To make the pastry, cream the butter, icing sugar and salt together in a bowl. Stir in the egg, then add the ground almonds and vanilla and mix well. Add the flour, and mix until just combined. Flatten the dough, wrap it in cling film (plastic wrap) and place in the fridge until firm.

When ready to proceed, preheat the oven to 200°C/180°C fan/400°F/Gas 6.

On a lightly floured work surface, roll out the dough to a circle about 3mm/⅛in thick. Line a 23cm/9in tart tin with the pastry and prick the base all over with a fork. Cover the pastry with a sheet of baking parchment and weigh it down with baking beans or dried rice. Bake for 15 minutes, then remove the tin from the oven, remove the baking beans and set aside.

While the pastry is baking, make the frangipane. Cream the butter and sugar together in a bowl until soft. Add the eggs and mix well. Stir in the almonds, vanilla and rum, if using, then mix in the cornflour.

Peel, halve and core the pears, then finely slice them crossways. Pour the frangipane into the tart case and arrange the pears on the top of the frangipane. Brush the pears with the melted butter and sprinkle over the sugar – this will help your pears keep their beautiful appearance when baked.

Return the filled tart to the oven for 25 minutes, or until the surface is golden brown. Enjoy warm.

Breton passion fruit and mango tart

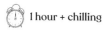 1 hour + chilling   30 minutes   🍴 8-10   2

For the passion fruit and lime curd

3–6 passion fruit

2–3 limes or lemons, juiced, plus the finely grated zest of 2 fruit

2 whole eggs, plus 1 egg yolk

100g/3½oz/½ cup caster (superfine) sugar

10g/⅓oz/1 tbsp cornflour (cornstarch)

50g/¾oz/3½ tbsp unsalted butter

For the tart base

185g/6½oz/¾ cup plus 1 tbsp butter, at room temperature

110g/3¾oz/¾ cup icing (confectioners') sugar

2 small egg yolks

160g/5¾oz/scant 1¼ cups plain (all-purpose) flour

55g/2oz/½ cup ground almonds

1 tsp vanilla extract

½ tsp salt

For the vanilla cream

200g/7oz/scant 1 cup double (heavy) cream

1 tbsp icing (confectioners') sugar

1 tsp vanilla bean paste or vanilla extract

For the mango topping

1 fully-ripe medium-sized mango

a few drops of lemon or lime juice

1 tsp vanilla bean paste or vanilla extract

½ tbsp icing (confectioners') sugar

This tart screams summer and makes a refreshing end to a meal. Don't be put off by the length of this recipe: I'm giving you useful options and detailed guidance. You'll find it's well worth your while.

Passion fruit costs a little more when not in season, so you can use anything from three to six passion fruit here and top up with lime or lemon juice as necessary to bring the total liquid to 120g/4¼oz/½ cup. The more passion fruit you add, the stronger its flavour will be. Blending your passion fruit pulp in one or two bursts using a hand blender, then straining it, will help you get the most juice from the fruit. Pick a mango that's ripe and fragrant.

To further minimise the cost of this dessert, you could swap the cream for a meringue made using the egg white left over from making the curd. I'm including a recipe for this in the tip overleaf: pick whichever works best for you. If you choose the meringue, blowtorching it before serving will add some extra decorative interest to your bake, but of course is not compulsory.

- -

It is a good idea to make the curd a few hours in advance, to give it time to set. Weigh the strained passion fruit pulp and add enough lemon or lime juice to bring the total weight to 120g/4¼oz/½ cup. Combine them in a small saucepan and place over a low heat.

Reserve about 1 teaspoon of the citrus zest for decoration and put the rest in a medium bowl with the eggs, egg yolk and sugar. Whisk until the sugar has dissolved, then add the cornflour and whisk again until fully blended.

Pour the hot fruit juice into the egg mixture in a slow, steady stream, whisking continuously. Return the mixture to the saucepan and heat, still whisking, until you have a very thick mixture. Remove from the heat, add the butter and whisk to emulsify (you could switch to an electric whisk or hand blender at this stage). Transfer the curd to a disposable piping bag and put in the fridge until set.

To make the tart base, follow the instructions for the Palets Bretons dough on page 82. Tip the finished dough onto a sheet of cling film (plastic wrap) and shape into a disc about 23cm/9in in diameter and 1cm/½in thick. Chill until the dough firms up (the freezer is faster than the fridge).

Meanwhile, preheat the oven to 180°C/160°C fan/350°F/Gas 4. Using a 23cm/9in tart tin like a cookie cutter, cut a disc to fit the tin. Put the pastry in the tin and bake for 30 minutes, or until golden

If you prefer, you could use a fabric piping bag fitted with a large round metal or plastic tip instead of disposable ones.

+ thrifty

If you'd like to make meringue instead of vanilla cream, put the 80g/2¾oz/ 7 tbsp sugar and 2 tbsp water in a small pan (in a large pan, too much will stick to the side and be wasted). Cook over a low heat until the syrup reaches 118°C/244°F or, if you don't have a thermometer, until the syrup is thicker but still clear and the bubbles rise more slowly.

When the syrup is nearly ready, use an electric hand whisk to whisk 1 egg white (about 40g/1½oz – use one left over from making the curd) with a drop of vinegar or a pinch of cream of tartar at high speed until foamy. When the syrup has reached the right temperature, pour it into the egg white in a slow and steady stream, whisking continuously. Keep whisking until the mixture has cooled completely, then place in a piping bag.

brown. Leave to cool in the tin for a few minutes, then turn out onto a wire rack to cool completely.

For the vanilla cream, use an electric whisk to whip the cream, sugar and vanilla together in a medium bowl until just stiff. Transfer to a disposable piping bag and chill until ready to assemble.

To make the topping, peel the mango using a sharp knife or potato peeler. Slice the flesh off the stone and dice into cubes. Place in a bowl and add a few drops of lemon or lime juice to stop your mango turning brown. Stir in the vanilla and icing sugar, then place in the fridge until ready to assemble.

Place your tart base on a presentation plate or board. Take your piping bag of whipped cream (or meringue) and cut a 2cm/¾in opening at the tip. Pipe thick blobs around the edge of the tart, pulling towards the centre as you finish. Repeat with a ring of curd blobs, starting where two of the whipped cream blobs are touching so they are offset to the cream. Fill the centre of the tart with the mango mixture and sprinkle with the reserved lime or lemon zest for colour. Enjoy cold.

Desserts

No-bake lime, basil and strawberry cheesecake

 30 minutes + chilling   none   12   1

For the base

250g/9oz oat biscuits (cookies) or digestive biscuits (graham crackers) (gf)

100g/3½oz/scant ½ cup butter, melted, plus extra for greasing

For the filling

1 x 397g/14oz can condensed milk

200g/7oz/scant 1 cup cream cheese

finely grated zest of 1 lime

50g/1¾oz/3½ tbsp lime juice

2 tbsp fresh basil leaves, finely chopped

1 tsp vanilla bean paste or extract

200g/7oz/scant 1 cup double (heavy) cream

To decorate

100g/3½oz strawberries (about 4 large strawberries)

1 tsp apricot jam (optional)

1 tsp water (optional)

a few small whole basil leaves (optional)

I love incorporating herbs in my sweet treats as they can be a great way to enhance the flavours of other ingredients. Basil pairs beautifully with strawberries, and adding lime makes this a great summer dessert you'll be proud to serve. It's quick to put together, too. You can add the strawberry decoration when you finish the cheesecake and the optional glaze will keep it looking fresh for a while. That said, because strawberries are fresh fruits, I like to add them just as I'm about to present the dessert, so those beautiful berries have maximum visual impact.

Grease a 20cm/8in loose-bottomed cake tin and line with baking parchment.

To make the base, blitz the biscuits in a food processor (or put them in a freezer bag and bash with a rolling pin, or similar) until you have a sandy powder. Tip them into a bowl, add the melted butter and mix well to combine. Transfer the mixture to the cake tin and press down firmly using the flat bottom of a glass. Put in the fridge to set for about 30 minutes.

For the filling, mix the condensed milk and cream cheese together in a bowl until smooth. Add the lime zest and juice, and the basil and vanilla, and mix well to combine. In a separate bowl, whip the cream until soft peaks form, taking care not to overwhip or it will start to curdle. Fold the whipped cream into the cream cheese mixture in two or three batches.

Take the biscuit base from the fridge and pour the cheesecake mixture evenly on top of it, smoothing the surface. Cover with cling film (plastic wrap) and return to the fridge to set for at least 12 hours, or overnight.

When ready to serve, cut the strawberries horizontally into thin slices. Starting from the outer rim of your cake, arrange the larger slices overlapping in a ring around the edge. Make a second ring inside this with the medium-sized slices, starting where two of the first row of strawberries join. Repeat the process towards the centre, using the smaller slices for the smaller rings in the middle, until the whole top is covered.

If you want to add some shine, make a glaze by melting a teaspoon of apricot jam with a teaspoon of water in the microwave for a few seconds, then brush it over the fruit. Finish with a few basil leaves, if you like.

Orange and cardamom crème brûlée

 30 minutes 30 minutes 8 2

600g/21oz/2½ cups double (heavy) cream
seeds from 8 cardamom pods
8 egg yolks
100g/3½oz/½ cup golden caster (superfine) sugar, plus 8 tsp extra to finish
50g/1¾oz/⅔ cup milk powder (optional)
1 tsp vanilla extract
finely grated zest of 2 large oranges

Crème brûlée uses a lot of egg yolks, so this is a recipe I often make when I stumble upon eggs on discount. You can freeze the egg whites to use later in cats' tongues on page 73, or for my chocolate and berry meringue roulade on page 136.

Orange zest and cardamom make this crème brûlée memorable and the powdered milk, while not compulsory, adds wonderful richness and creaminess.

- -

Preheat the oven to 170°C/150°C fan/325°F/Gas 3.

Put the cream and cardamom seeds in a medium saucepan. Bring to a simmer, then immediately remove from the heat and set aside to infuse for about 10 minutes.

In bowl, whisk the egg yolks and sugar together until light and fluffy. Add the milk powder, if using.

Pour the infused cream onto the egg mixture in a slow, steady stream, whisking continuously. Pour the custard back into the pan through a fine-meshed sieve to remove the cardamom seeds. Stir in the vanilla and orange zest.

Return the pan to a low heat and cook, stirring continuously, until the custard thickens slightly. If you have a thermometer, you want your custard to reach 83°C/181°F. Otherwise, run your finger across the back of the coated spoon – the custard is ready when it leaves a clear trail.

Find yourself eight small–medium ramekin dishes. Remove the pan from the heat and pour the custard into your ramekins. Place your ramekins in a high-sided roasting tray. Fill the tray with hot water from the kettle until it comes about two-thirds up the sides of the ramekins. Carefully transfer the tray to the oven and bake for 30 minutes, or until the custard is just set but still a little wobbly in the middle.

Using oven gloves, carefully remove the tray from the oven, lift the ramekins from the tray and set them aside to cool at room temperature. Once cool, cover the ramekins with cling film (plastic wrap) or foil and store them in the fridge until you are almost ready to eat.

To finish the brûlées, sprinkle a teaspoon of sugar over the top of each custard and caramelize using a blowtorch. If you don't have a blowtorch, follow my tip (left).

+ tip

If you don't have a blowtorch, you can make a hard caramel, pour it over a silicone mat and allow it to cool and harden. Crack the caramel all over, then put the pieces in a food processor and blend to a fine powder. Dust your chilled crème brûlées with this powder and place them under a hot grill (broiler) to melt. Leave to cool before serving.

Apple compote crumble

 30 minutes   30 minutes | 8   1

900g/2lb apples (about 8 apples), peeled, cored and diced
2 tbsp lemon juice (optional)
200g/7oz/1 cup light brown sugar
100g/3½oz/scant ½ cup unsalted butter
1 tsp vanilla bean paste or vanilla extract
a pinch of salt
custard or ice cream, to serve (optional)

For the crumble

100g/3½oz/¾ cup plain (all-purpose) flour (gf)
100g/3½oz/½ cup light brown sugar
50g/1¾oz/3½ tbsp cold unsalted butter
50g/1¾oz/½ cup rolled oats (gf)
1 tsp vanilla bean paste or vanilla extract
a pinch of salt

Apples keep for a long time in the fridge or freezer. Choosing those in season will help save a few pennies and freezing your favourites when they're on offer is a great way to ensure you can enjoy them throughout the year too.

This crumble is a great way to use fresh or frozen apples and works very well as a single bake or as individual desserts in ramekins. Butter in the apple sauce makes it moreish and absolutely delicious to eat on its own. I've kept the filling simply flavoured with vanilla, but you could add cinnamon or other spices such as cloves, ginger and nutmeg. Although optional, a little lemon juice will help prevent your apples browning.

- -

To make the crumble, put all the ingredients in a mixing bowl and rub them between your fingers until they're well combined and crumbly. Chill until ready to use.

To make the apple compote, put the diced apples in a large bowl, add the lemon juice, if using, and mix well to prevent oxidation, which will start to turn your apples brown.

Transfer half the apples to a saucepan. Add the sugar and butter and cook over a medium heat for about 15 minutes, or until the apples are soft and their liquid has reduced slightly. Use a hand blender to purée the cooked apples, then stir the uncooked apple cubes into the purée along with the vanilla.

Spoon the apple compote into an ovenproof dish or individual ramekins. Sprinkle over the crumble and bake at 220°C/200°C fan/425°F/Gas 7 for 30 minutes, or until the crumble is golden. Enjoy warm with custard or ice cream, if wished.

Chocolate crémeux and salted caramel dessert

 40 minutes + chilling    20 minutes   8   1

For the genoise

20g/⅔oz/2 tbsp cornflour (cornstarch)

40g/1½oz/4¾ tbsp plain (all-purpose) flour (or skip the cornflour and use 60g/2oz/7¼ tbsp plain flour) *(gf plus ⅛ tsp xanthan gum)*

30g/1oz/scant ⅓ cup unsweetened cocoa powder

¼ tsp baking powder *(gf)* (optional)

3 large eggs (55g/2oz each)

100g/3½oz/½ cup caster (superfine) sugar

30g/1oz/2 tbsp butter, melted, plus extra for greasing

a pinch of salt

For the syrup

50g/1¾oz/¼ cup caster (superfine) sugar

50g/1¾oz/3½ tbsp water

For the salted caramel

1 tbsp water

50g/1¾oz/¼ cup caster (superfine) sugar

15g/½oz/1 tbsp butter

50g/1¾oz/3½ tbsp double (heavy) cream

a pinch of salt

½ tsp vanilla extract

For the crémeux

110g/3¾oz/scant ½ cup milk

110g/3¾oz/scant ½ cup double (heavy) cream

60g/2oz/5 tbsp caster (superfine) sugar

2 egg yolks

100g/3½oz dark (bittersweet) chocolate, chopped into small pieces

½ tsp coffee powder

This is a simple and beautiful dessert that won't disappoint any chocolate lovers.

- -

Preheat the oven to 200°C/180°C fan/400°F/Gas 6. Grease a 20cm/8in cake tin and line with baking parchment.

Make a genoise batter following the method for the Black Forest gateau on page 142. Pour it into your prepared cake tin and bake for 20 minutes.

Meanwhile, prepare the syrup. Combine the sugar and water in a small pan and bring to a boil. Take off the heat and set aside to cool.

While your genoise is cooling, make the salted caramel. Put the water in a small saucepan and add the sugar. Cook over medium heat to a medium-to-dark amber colour, taking care not to burn the caramel. Add the butter and stir until incorporated. Mix in the cream and, when fully combined, remove from the heat. Stir in the salt and vanilla, then set aside to cool and thicken slightly.

For the crémeux, put the milk and cream in a saucepan and bring to scalding point. In a separate bowl, whisk the sugar and egg yolks. Pour the milk mixture slowly over the egg mixture while continuously mixing. Return the mixture to the saucepan and place over a low heat – you don't want the mixture to boil and become grainy. Mix continuously until the mixture thickens; when you swipe your finger over the back of the coated spatula, the track should remain. Pour the custard over the chopped chocolate and allow to sit for a few minutes, then stir the mixture until you get a smooth cream. Press cling film (plastic wrap) over the surface of the crémeux, and place in the fridge for at least 2 hours to cool down and firm up.

To assemble the cake, place the genoise on your cake plate. Using a pastry brush, soak the genoise with the syrup. Put the crémeux in a piping bag fitted with a nozzle of your choice – or switching between nozzles can add interest too. Pipe some big blobs on top of the cake. Place a teaspoon in some hot water to heat it and wipe off the excess water. Place the back of the spoon on top of each blob to create a dip, reheating the spoon in the water if necessary.

Spoon about 1 teaspoon of the salted caramel into each dip. If you find your caramel too thick to handle, warm it up in the microwave for 10 seconds, but not too hot or it will melt the crémaux. For a simpler decoration, just drizzle the caramel on top of the crémeux.

Place the dessert in the fridge until ready to serve. Keep refrigerated in an airtight container for up to 3 days.

Chocolate and hazelnut cream pie

 50 minutes + chilling   none   12   2

For the crust

450g/1lb cookies and cream
  biscuits (such as Oreos) *(gf)*
120g/4¼oz/½ cup butter, melted

For the filling

350g/12oz/1½ cups plus 2 tsp
  full-fat cream cheese
200g/7oz/¾ cup plus 2 tbsp
  hazelnut chocolate spread
1 tsp vanilla extract
100g/3½oz/¾ cup icing
  (confectioner's) sugar
200g/7oz/¾ cup plus 2 tbsp
  double (heavy) cream

For the topping

150g/5½oz/⅔ cup hazelnut
  chocolate spread
100g/3½oz/scant ½ cup double
  (heavy) cream
10g/⅓oz/1 rounded tbsp icing
  (confectioners') sugar
3 cookies and cream biscuits,
  quartered, *(gf)* or 12 pieces of
  chocolate of your choice, to
  decorate

This cookie and cream pie is so easy to make and you won't even need an oven as there is no baking involved. When it comes to decorating your cream pie, you can make use of all those leftover Easter eggs. I like it just as it is – not overly sweet – but if you would like to add more sweetness to it, you could even crush a few of those chocolate Easter eggs in the cream mixture. If you don't have any Easter eggs to decorate the top of your pie, you could leave it just with the piped rosettes, or add a few of the cookies and cream biscuits on top.

Crush the cookies and cream biscuits – either in a food processor or in a freezer bag and using a rolling pin, or similar – until you have a sandy mixture. Scoop out 1 tablespoon of the mixture and set it aside for later. Add the melted butter to the remaining crumbs and mix until combined.

Tip the mixture into a 20cm/8in loose-bottomed cake tin and use a tall glass to press it down firmly into the bottom and up the side of the tin. Refrigerate for at least 1 hour, or until it sets.

Once the base has set, put the cream cheese, chocolate spread, vanilla and icing sugar in a mixing bowl and whip until smooth.

In a separate bowl, whip the double cream to just soft peaks. Fold the whipped cream into the cream cheese mixture in two batches. Pour the mixture into cake tin and level the top using a spatula.

For the topping, melt the chocolate spread for 10–20 seconds in the microwave, just so it is easily spreadable but not hot. Pour the hazelnut spread on top of the cream cheese filling and spread evenly. Return to the fridge while preparing the rest of the toppings.

In a small bowl, whip the cream for the topping with the icing sugar to stiff peaks. Place in a piping bag with a nozzle of your choice. (Or improvise using a piping bag made with parchment paper, with the tip cut like a star nozzle – see page 13.) Pipe 12 rosettes around the edge of the cake. Top each rosette with a piece of cookies and cream biscuit, or use a square of chocolate, chocolate Easter egg of your choice or just leave plain. Sprinkle the reserved 1 tablespoon of crushed biscuits in a circle in the middle – for a neat circle, you can use a cookie cutter as a guide. Refrigerate for at least 4 hours.

When ready to serve, unmould the cake onto a serving plate – using a warm damp kitchen towel to wipe the outside edge of your cake tin will help release the pie easily. Store it in an airtight container in the fridge for up to 3 days.

Spiced pineapple and coconut crumble

 30 minutes 30 minutes | 8 [2]

1kg/2lb 4oz pineapple (1 large or
   2 medium-sized pineapples)
100g/3½oz/½ cup light brown
   sugar
15g/½oz/1½ tbsp cornflour
   (cornstarch)
1 tbsp ground cinnamon
½ tsp ground ginger
¼ tsp ground nutmeg
¼ tsp ground allspice
2 tbsp rum (optional)
50g/1¾oz/3½ tbsp butter, melted,
   plus extra for greasing
vanilla ice cream, to serve

For the crumble

100g/3½oz/1⅓ cups desiccated
   (dried shredded) coconut
200g/7oz/1½ cups plain
   (all-purpose) flour (gf)
200g/7oz/1 cup butter
150g/5½oz/¾ cup sugar
½ tsp salt
50g/1¾oz/½ cup rolled oats (gf)

+ thrifty

You don't have to throw
the pineapple core
away. Roughly chop it
and pop it in a blender
or food processor. Blitz to
a smooth purée and you
can now freeze it in an
ice cube tray and add to
smoothies or use it in the
carrot cake recipe (see
page 126).

My parents owned a pineapple farm so when I was young, they
were everywhere! No surprise, then, that this tropical dessert
reminds me of home and growing up.

Pineapple works incredibly well with cinnamon and nutmeg,
and the addition of sugar and butter creates a toffee-like base that
I like to round off with a splash of rum. As always, you can omit it,
but I feel a few drops add a little something to this dessert and the
alcohol mostly evaporates by the time the crumble is cooked. Oats
and desiccated coconut (toast it while preheating your oven) add
crunch to the topping, making this a great combination of flavours
and textures.

You want to choose a *ripe* pineapple – it makes a massive
difference. Ripe pineapple is naturally sweet and packed with
flavour. When pineapple is ready, it smells aromatic, the skin turns
yellow-brown, and you can pull the leaves out easily. You could, of
course, use canned or frozen pineapple if that's what's available,
but will need to adjust the sugar to taste. Here in the UK, you can
often buy a fresh pineapple cheaper than a canned or frozen one
– and they are available year-round, so it makes sense to choose
fresh! The greengrocer is often a cheaper place to get them than
the supermarket.

- -

Preheat your oven to 200°C/180°C fan/400°F/Gas 6 and generously
grease a baking dish with butter. If you like, while the oven's heating
you can briefly toast the desiccated coconut for the crumble
topping on a baking tray.

Peel your pineapple, removing the eyes and core (see tip, left), and
cut it into 1.5cm/⅝in cubes. Place in a large bowl and set aside.

In a separate bowl, combine the brown sugar, cornflour and spices
and give them a good mix. Tip the mixture over the pineapple and
mix well to combine. Add the rum, if using, and mix well. Drizzle
over the melted butter and give it a final mix, then tip the mixture
into the prepared baking dish, and set aside.

To make the crumble topping, in a separate bowl combine the flour,
butter, sugar and salt. Rub them between your fingers to a sandy
texture, then stir in the oats and desiccated coconut.

Sprinkle the crumble topping over your pineapple mixture and bake
for 30 minutes or until the crumble is golden. Leave the crumble to
cool at room temperature for 20 minutes before serving warm with
a scoop of vanilla ice cream.

No-churn wild blackberry and biscuit ice cream cake

 20 minutes + freezing   none   12 1

200g/7oz/1⅓ cups blackberries
1 tbsp sugar
1 tsp lemon juice
finely grated zest of ½ lemon
200g/7oz digestive biscuits
  (graham crackers) (gf), or see
  tip below
80g/2¾oz/⅓ cup butter, melted
1 x 397g/14oz can condensed milk
1 tbsp vanilla extract
600g/21oz/2½ cups whipping
  cream or double (heavy) cream

I love making my own ice cream – it's a great activity to indulge in at home with kids. As the name suggests, this no-churn ice cream does not require an ice cream maker and is super-simple to put together. It has a crunchy biscuit base filled with delicious vanilla ice cream, marbled with blackberry ripple made from fruit that I forage from the brambles at the back of my garden.

This is one of those penny-saving recipes to make when you stumble upon discounted double cream at the supermarket. You can omit the blackberries and make a simple vanilla ice cream, or use it as a base for any other fruit coulis you like: mangoes and coconut or raspberries and/or strawberries when in season, would be a few suggestions. You can even substitute chocolate or marshmallows for the berries.

- -

Put the blackberries in a saucepan with the sugar and the lemon juice and zest. Cook on medium–low heat for about 5 minutes, or until the blackberries break down and the mixture thickens to a loose coulis. Set aside to cool.

Line a 900g/2lb loaf tin (or a plastic box of similar size and shape) with baking parchment to help you lift out the ice cream once frozen. You can also use a loose-based 20cm/8in round cake tin.

Put the biscuits in a plastic food bag and bash them with a rolling pin or similar to crush them. Once they are crumbs, tip them into a bowl, add the melted butter and stir until combined. Tip the mixture into the prepared tin and spread it level, then press it down firmly and place in the fridge to set.

Put the condensed milk and vanilla in a bowl and mix well.

In a separate bowl, whip the cream until it almost holds firm peaks – take care not to overwhip or it will curdle. Gently fold the whipped cream into the condensed milk a little at a time until fully incorporated.

Pour half the cream mixture onto the biscuit base. Drizzle with half the blackberry coulis and swirl it in using a knife. Pour over the remaining cream mixture and repeat the process with the rest of the blackberry coulis to make a pretty swirl on top. Place in the freezer until firm.

To serve, lift the ice cream from the tin using the edges of the paper to help. Transfer the ice cream to a plate, peel away the paper, and allow to soften at room temperature before slicing into it.

+ tip

You can also try substituting the digestive biscuits with ones of your choice, such as speculoos or Oreos, or recipes from this book such as the sablé biscuits (see page 71) or cookie dough (see page 85).

Fancy a carrot cake

 40 minutes, plus chilling 25 minutes 8

120g/4¼oz/1 cup less 1½ tbsp plain
(all-purpose) flour *(gf)*

1 tsp baking powder *(gf)*

½ tsp bicarbonate of soda (baking
soda)

¼ tsp ground cinnamon

½ tsp ground ginger

a pinch of ground nutmeg

¼ tsp salt

1 large egg

50g/1¾oz/3½ tbsp sunflower oil,
or vegetable oil, plus extra for
greasing

50g/1¾oz/¼ cup golden caster or
white caster (superfine) sugar

50g/1¾oz/¼ cup pineapple purée
or crushed pineapple

½ tsp finely grated orange zest,
plus 30g/1oz/2 tbsp juice from
the orange

1 tsp vanilla bean paste or extract

100g/3½oz finely grated carrot

For the carrot jam

150g/5½oz carrots, finely grated

150g/5½oz/¾ cup jam sugar or
caster (superfine) sugar

¼ tsp finely grated orange zest,
plus 15g/½oz/1 tbsp orange juice

¼ tsp finely grated lemon zest,
plus 15g/½oz/1 tbsp lemon juice

100g/3½oz/scant ½ cup water

1 tsp vanilla bean paste or extract

For the frosting

100g/3½oz white chocolate

200g/7oz/¾ cup plus 2 tbsp
cream cheese

1 tsp vanilla bean paste or extract

170g/6oz/¾ cup double (heavy)
cream

25g/1oz/2¾ tbsp icing
(confectioners') sugar

Even as a thrifty baker, there are times when we have a special occasion and want to make a dessert with a little something extra to please that crowd.

It's the carrot jam that makes this cake special, and it can be made a few days in advance. I've used jam sugar because the pectin in it gives the jam a shiny, jelly-like appearance, but if you don't have any, use ordinary caster sugar. After all, being thrifty is about making do with what we have.

You could, of course, choose to serve this as a simple carrot cake without the carrot bow. But hopefully, this recipe shows how your choice of design – even when it's simple – can really make a cake pop. The bow is made with fresh raw carrots, so after a day or so they dehydrate and tend to look flatter and less plump – bear this in mind and make sure the bow is made and added at the last minute.

- -

To make the carrot cake, preheat the oven to 190°C/170°C fan/ 375°F/Gas 5. Grease and line a 20cm/8in round cake tin with baking parchment and set aside.

In a large bowl, mix together the flour, baking powder, bicarbonate of soda, ground spices and salt and set aside. In another bowl, whisk together the egg, oil, sugar, pineapple, orange zest and juice, and vanilla until fully combined. Add the wet ingredients to the dry ingredients and stir until well combined. Fold in the grated carrot until fully incorporated.

Pour the batter into the prepared cake tin and bake for 25 minutes, or until a skewer inserted into the centre of the cake comes out clean. Allow to cool in the tin for a few minutes before turning out onto a wire rack to cool completely before assembling the cake – this is very important!

To make the carrot jam, put the carrots, sugar, citrus zests and juices and water in a saucepan and bring to a boil. Reduce the heat to low and allow the mixture to slowly reduce until the consistency is syrupy, then stir in the vanilla. If you'll be using the jam straight away, pour it into a glass bowl and set aside to cool. Otherwise, pour it into a sterilised jar, add the screw lid and turn it upside down.

To make the frosting, melt the white chocolate in the microwave in 10-second bursts, stirring in between, or melt it in a double boiler.

Ingredients continue overleaf...

To decorate (optional)

1 whole large carrot
1 tsp apricot jam
1 tsp water

Put the cream cheese in a bowl with the vanilla, add the white chocolate and whip until smooth. In a separate bowl, whip the double cream with the icing sugar just until firm peaks start to form – you don't want it too soft as your mixture won't set, but nor do you want to whisk it all the way to stiff peaks as it will start to curdle by the time you pipe or spread it. Fold the whipped cream into the cream cheese mixture in two batches. If you want to go all the way and decorate your cake with the bow, set aside 2 tablespoons of the frosting to use as a glue later.

Cut a strip of baking parchment or acetate double the height of your cake and long enough to fit around it. Wrap the paper or acetate around the cake and secure with some tape. Pour the carrot jam over the top and level it with a palette knife. Pour the frosting on top of the jam and smooth the surface. Place in the fridge to set for a couple of hours.

Remove the baking parchment and neaten the edge with a spatula if necessary. You can enjoy the cake now, as it is, because from here onward, all is vanity! Nonetheless, it's worth it.

To decorate the cake, peel several fine long strips from the whole carrot using a potato peeler. Using a spatula, place about 1 tablespoon of the reserved frosting at the centre of the cake. Join the ends of one carrot ribbon to make a loop, and glue the ends onto the frosting. Repeat with the other carrot ribbons until you have a beautiful bow. Refrigerate until almost ready to serve.

Take the cake out of the fridge a few minutes before serving. If you have some apricot jam, melt a teaspoon of it with a teaspoon of water. Use a pastry brush to gently brush it over the bow to make it shine.

Special
Occasions

Peanut butter cake

 1 hour 35 minutes ⫙ 12 (or 24 cupcakes) 1

250g/9oz/1¾ cups plus 2 tbsp
   plain (all-purpose) flour (gf plus
   ½ tsp xanthan gum)
350g/12oz/1¾ cups caster
   (superfine) sugar
50g/1¾oz/½ cup cocoa powder
2 tsp baking powder (gf)
1 tsp bicarbonate of soda (baking
   soda)
¼ tsp salt
2 large eggs
100g/3½oz/scant ½ cup vegetable
   oil, plus extra for greasing
280g/10oz/1¼ cups milk
2 tsp vanilla extract
1½ tsp coffee powder
200g/7oz/¾ cup plus 2 tbsp
   hot water
150g/5½oz/1½ cups crushed
   roasted salted peanuts

For the caramel

150g/5½oz/¾ cup caster
   (superfine) sugar
50g/1¾oz/3½ tbsp water
40g/1½oz/3 tbsp butter
180g/6¼oz/¾ cup double (heavy)
   cream
a pinch of salt
1 tsp vanilla extract

For the peanut butter frosting

200g/7oz/¾ cup plus 2 tbsp
   peanut butter
250g/9oz/1 cup plus 2 tbsp butter,
   at soft room temperature
300g/10½oz/2 cups plus 2 tbsp
   icing (confectioners') sugar
80g/2¾oz/⅓ cup double (heavy)
   cream
2 tsp vanilla extract
¼ tsp salt

Ingredients continue overleaf...

If you are a peanut butter lover, you will approve of this one. While I have presented this cake as a celebration cake, you can also choose to make a cupcake version of it.

Baking these in cupcake version is a big thrift flex because smaller cakes bake in a shorter amount of time. Because they are pre-portioned, the same amount of cake batter will serve more people. You will get 12 slices out of the celebration cake, but about 24 cupcakes. You also won't need the chocolate ganache dripping. See the tip on page 132 for the method.

Preheat the oven to 200°C/180°C fan/400°F/Gas 6. Grease three 20cm/8in cake tins and line them with baking parchment.

Put the flour, sugar, cocoa powder, baking powder, bicarbonate of soda and salt in a bowl. Mix well and set aside.

In a separate bowl, whisk the eggs, then add the oil, milk and vanilla and mix until fully combined. Pour this mixture over the dry ingredients and mix to combine. Add the coffee to the hot water and pour over the batter in small batches while continuously mixing.

Divide the batter evenly between the cake tins, then place all three tins in the oven. Bake for 30–35 minutes, or until a skewer inserted into the centre of the cakes comes out clean. Leave to cool in the tins for a few minutes, then transfer them to a wire rack to cool completely.

For the caramel, put the water in a saucepan and add the sugar to it. Cook to a medium-to-dark amber colour, taking care not to burn the caramel. Add the butter and stir until incorporated, then mix in the cream. When fully combined, remove the pan from the heat and stir in the salt and vanilla. Set aside to cool and thicken slightly.

For the peanut butter frosting, put the peanut butter, butter and icing sugar in a bowl. Mix on low speed to bring all the ingredients together, then increase the speed and mix until light and fluffy. Stop to scrape the sides of the bowl if needed. Add the cream, vanilla and salt and whip for about a minute.

To make the chocolate drip ganache, melt the chocolate and double cream together in the microwave in 30-second bursts, stirring in between. Set aside to cool slightly.

To assemble the cake, spread a teaspoon of the frosting onto your cake board or cake stand. Place the first cake sponge on top to

For the chocolate drip

100g/3½oz dark chocolate
130g/4½oz/generous ½ cup
double (heavy) cream

+tip

for 24 cupcakes:

If making cupcakes,
line two 12-hole muffin
tins with paper cases.
Follow the method on
the previous page to
make the batter and fill
each muffin case two-
thirds full. Bake at the
same temperature for
15–20 minutes. Remove
from the oven and allow
to cool for 20 minutes,
then unmould from the
tins and allow to cool
completely.

To decorate, fit your
piping bag with a star
nozzle (or see page 13
for how to improvise).
Fill the bag with the
peanut frosting and
pipe a rosette on top
of each cupcake. Skip
the chocolate ganache,
but generously drizzle
some salted caramel
over each cupcake and
finish with a sprinkle of
crushed peanuts.

secure it on the base. Spoon about one-fifth of the frosting on top and spread around evenly. Spread one-third of the caramel in a circle in the centre (stopping about 2cm/¾in before the edge of the cake) and sprinkle one-third of the crushed peanuts over the caramel.

Place the second sponge on top and repeat the process, adding another one-fifth of the frosting, followed by another one-third each of the caramel and crushed peanuts. Place the final sponge on the top. Spoon another one-fifth of the frosting on top and spread around evenly. Use the remaining two-fifths of the frosting to cover the sides of the cake.

Using the remaining caramel, create a drip effect by carefully pouring caramel around the top rim of the cake and, at intervals, pushing it over the top and allowing it to drizzle down the side. Leave enough gap between each drip to add a drip of the chocolate.

Pour two-thirds of the chocolate dripping on top of the cake and spread it evenly to the edge with a palette knife. Use the remaining chocolate dripping to create a drip effect, pushing the chocolate over the edge so that a drip is created between each caramel drip, so that they alternate around the cake. Sprinkle the remaining crushed peanuts in a ring around the edge of the cake. Place in the fridge until ready to enjoy. Remove from the fridge about 30 minutes before serving.

Store the cake in the fridge for up to 5 days.

Moka cake

 1 hour 50 minutes 10–30 minutes (depending on your choice of tin) 12 2

For the genoise

50g/1¾oz/½ cup cornflour
  (cornstarch)
120g/4¼oz/1 cup less 1½ tbsp plain
  (all-purpose) flour (gf plus
  ¼ tsp xanthan gum)
5g/⅛oz/1½ tsp baking powder (gf)
  (optional – see page 19)
¼ tsp salt
5 large eggs
170g/6oz/¾ cup plus 1½ tbsp
  caster (superfine) sugar
1 tsp vanilla extract

For the coffee syrup

100g/3½oz/½ cup caster
  (superfine) sugar
100g/3½oz/scant ½ cup hot water
1 tbsp instant coffee powder
  (use decaf, if preferred)

For the buttercream

250g/9oz/1¼ cups caster
  (superfine) sugar
80g/2¾oz/⅓ cup water
3 large eggs
450g/1lb/2 cups butter, at room
  temperature
1 tbsp instant coffee powder
  dissolved in ½ tbsp hot water

To decorate

60g/2oz/¾ cup almond flakes,
  toasted
20g/⅔oz dark (bittersweet)
  chocolate, melted
chocolate balls or chocolate-
  coated coffee beans (optional)

A moka is a French cake, one that was always displayed in patisserie windows when I was growing up and a favourite choice for birthdays – alongside vanilla cake and Black Forest gateau.

It's made from layers of genoise sponge soaked in coffee syrup and sandwiched with coffee-flavoured French buttercream. It is believed that French buttercream was first invented in 1865 by a French baker called Quillet and his first version was made with egg yolk. There have been so many variants since then, but we are not about to waste anything here so we will use the whole egg – I'm sure you have enough whites in your freezer by now! The egg is cooked by the hot sugar syrup so don't be alarmed at the prospect of eating raw egg.

You could bake this genoise in a baking tray and turn it into a yule log at Christmas time; if you like, you can add a little brandy to the coffee syrup for a bit of festive oomph.

- -

Preheat your oven to 200°C/180°C fan/400°F/Gas 6. Grease a deep 22cm/8½in round cake tin (or three shallow 22cm/8½in tins, if you wish to bake the layers separately) and line with baking parchment.

Sift the flours and baking powder (if using) into a mixing bowl, add the salt and set aside.

Put the eggs and sugar in a mixing bowl and whisk with an electric hand mixer for 10 minutes, or until the mixture triples in size and falls from the whisk in a smooth ribbon.

Sprinkle the flour mixture over the egg mixture in two stages, folding in each batch with three or four turns of a small balloon whisk (you can use a spatula, but the balloon whisk will help keep more air in the mixture). Add the vanilla and fold in gently.

Pour the batter into the prepared cake tin(s). If baking in three tins, cook for 10–12 minutes; or for 30 minutes if using a single cake tin. The genoise is done when a skewer inserted into the centre comes out clean. Unmould the cake(s) onto a wire rack and allow to cool completely.

While your cake is baking, prepare the coffee syrup by combining the sugar, hot water and coffee in a small pan. Bring to a boil, stirring, then remove from the heat and set aside to cool.

To make the buttercream, put the sugar and water in a saucepan and heat to 118°C/244°F. If you don't have a sugar thermometer, cook until the bubbles have slowed down, and the sugar syrup is thick but still clear.

If you have them,
dividing the cake batter
into three shallow cake
tins will mean a much
shorter baking time,
saving you energy.

+ tip

It is best to make the
buttercream just as you
are ready to assemble
the cake. If you make it in
advance and put it in the
fridge, it will solidify and
you will then need to
leave it to stand at room
temperature and whip it
again before using.

Using an electric whisk or a stand mixer fitted with the balloon attachment, whisk the eggs on high speed until frothy – about 1 minute. Reduce the speed to medium and pour in the syrup in a slow, steady stream, whisking continuously. If the speed is too high, the syrup will splash on the side of the bowl and not into the egg mixture. Once all the syrup is incorporated, increase the speed and whisk until the mixture is light and fluffy and has cooled completely (or to about 20°C/68°F) – this is so the butter does not melt when incorporated.

Add the soft butter a tablespoon at a time, whisking continuously and waiting until the butter is fully incorporated before adding more. Add the dissolved coffee and keep whisking until the buttercream is light and creamy.

If you baked the genoise in one tin, slice the cooled cake horizontally into three layers. To assemble, place your first layer on a flat plate or cake board. Soak it with a third of the cold coffee syrup, using a pastry brush or spoon. Add a few scoops of buttercream (about 80g/2¾oz) and spread it over the cake using a knife or spatula.

Place the second layer of sponge on top and soak it with half the remaining syrup. Spread another 80g/2¾oz of buttercream over the surface. Add the final layer of sponge, soak with the remaining syrup and spread another 80g/2¾oz of buttercream on top. Using a serrated knife or cake scraper, create some zigzag patterns on top of the cake.

Next, smooth a couple of tablespoons of the remaining buttercream over the sides of the cake and and press the toasted almond flakes into it to cover the sides.

Put the remaining cream into a piping bag fitted with a star nozzle (or see page 13 to improvise). Pipe some rosettes around the top of the cake.

Put the melted chocolate into a piping bag, cut a tiny piece from the tip and write the word 'Moka' – or a special message of your choice – on top of your cake. Decorate with the chocolate balls or chocolate-coated coffee beans, if using, and serve. If you need to refrigerate it to serve another time, remember the cake will solidify in the fridge, so leave it to stand at room temperature for 30–40 minutes before slicing.

Chocolate and berry meringue roulade

 1 hour 30 minutes 12 1

For the berry compote

150g/5½oz frozen mixed berries, thawed, plus extra frozen ones to decorate

2 tsp lemon juice

1 tbsp caster (superfine) sugar

10g/⅓oz/1½ tbsp cornflour (cornstarch)

For the meringue

30g/1oz/¼ cup cornflour (cornstarch)

15g/½oz/1½ tbsp unsweetened cocoa powder

½ tsp instant coffee powder (optional)

4 egg whites (total weight 150g/5½oz)

½ tsp white vinegar

240g/8½oz/1¼ cups caster (superfine) sugar

For the chocolate cream filling

100g/3½oz dark chocolate

200ml/7fl oz/scant 1 cup double (heavy) cream

200g/7oz/scant 1 cup full-fat cream cheese

30g/1oz/3½ tbsp icing (confectioners') sugar, plus extra to dust

+ tip

When making the chocolate cream filling, make sure you pour the cream onto the chocolate and not the other way round. Adding the chocolate to the cream will solidify your chocolate and give the cream a grainy appearance.

Meringue roulades are a great way to use those egg whites that you have been saving. This is a great cake for the festive season, but it can also be adapted for summer by omitting the cocoa powder and replacing the berries with a lemon or raspberry curd.

- -

To make the compote, put the berries, lemon juice, sugar and cornflour in a jug or bowl and blend to a purée. Pour the mixture into a saucepan, place over a low heat and stir until the purée has thickened. Pour into a shallow dish, cover the surface with cling film (plastic wrap) and leave to cool completely.

Meanwhile, preheat the oven to 200°C/180°C fan/400°F/Gas 6. Line a rimmed 33 x 22cm/13 x 8½in baking tray with baking parchment.

To make the meringue, sift together the cornflour, cocoa powder and coffee (if using) and set aside.

Using a clean bowl and an electric hand whisk, beat the egg whites and vinegar together until stiff. Add the sugar 1 tablespoon at a time, whisking continuously, until the meringue is thick and glossy and stiff peaks form when the whisk is lifted from the bowl. Use a spatula to fold in the cocoa mixture until fully incorporated. Spread out the meringue evenly in the lined baking tray. Bake for 10 minutes, before lowering the temperature to 180°C/160°C fan/350°F/Gas 4 and continuing to bake for another 20 minutes.

Lay a clean kitchen towel on the work surface. Cover with a sheet of baking parchment, then tip the cooked meringue onto it. Without removing the paper, allow it to cool completely for an hour or so.

To make the cream filling, melt the chocolate in a large bowl set over a pan of simmering water (or in the microwave) and allow to cool slightly. Pour the cream onto the chocolate in a slow, steady stream, whipping continuously until stiff peaks form. In a separate bowl, beat the cream cheese and icing sugar together until smooth, then fold in the chocolate cream until fully incorporated.

To assemble, remove the parchment from the meringue. Spread three-quarters of the filling evenly over it, leaving a 3cm/1¼in strip bare along a short edge. Spread the compote over the cream filling, then roll up the meringue towards the bare edge.

Fit a piping bag with a St-Honoré nozzle (or improvise using the instructions on page 13) and fill with the remaining cream filling. Pipe the cream in a zig zag down the length of the top of the roulade. Chill for a minimum of 2 hours before decorating with frozen berries and dusting with icing sugar just before serving.

Semi-naked strawberry cake

 50 minutes   15 minutes   12   2

For the genoise
60g/2oz/heaped ½ cup cornflour
(cornstarch)
120g/4¼oz/1 cup less 1½ tbsp plain
(all-purpose) flour (gf plus ¼ tsp
xanthan gum)
1 tsp baking powder (gf) (optional)
a large pinch of salt
6 eggs
180g/6¼oz/1 cup less 1½ tbsp
caster (superfine) sugar
2 tsp vanilla bean paste or vanilla
extract
60g/2oz/¼ cup butter, melted,
plus extra for greasing

For the syrup
100g/3½oz/½ cup caster
(superfine) sugar
100g/3½oz/7 tbsp water
1 tbsp rum or brandy (optional),
or 1 tsp vanilla bean paste or
vanilla extract

For the cream
250g/9oz/1 cup mascarpone
cheese
40g/1½oz/3¼ tbsp caster
(superfine) sugar
250g/9oz/1 cup double (heavy)
cream
40g/1½oz/4½ tbsp icing
(confectioner's) sugar
2 tsp vanilla bean paste or extract
a pinch of salt

For the chocolate drip (optional)
30g/1oz dark (bittersweet) chocolate
50g/1¾oz/3½ tbsp double (heavy)
cream

To fill and decorate
200g/7oz strawberries, left whole,
plus 100g/3½oz extra, sliced
other berries of choice (optional)

The perfect cake for a summer garden party or to celebrate a family birthday, this is one of my all-time favourites.

Preheat the oven to 200°C/180°C fan/400°F/Gas 6. Grease three 20cm/8in round cake tins and line with baking parchment.

Sift the flours and baking powder (if using), into a mixing bowl. Add the salt and set aside.

Put the eggs and sugar in a mixing bowl and whisk with an electric hand mixer for 10 minutes, or until the mixture triples in size and falls from the whisk in a smooth ribbon. Sprinkle the sifted flours over the egg mixture in two stages, folding in each batch with three or four turns of a small balloon whisk (the whisk will help keep more air in the mixture). Add the vanilla and melted butter and fold in gently.

Divide the batter between the prepared tins. Bake all three at once for 15 minutes, or until a skewer inserted into the centre comes out clean. Unmould the sponges onto a wire rack to cool completely.

While your cakes are baking, prepare the syrup by combining the sugar and water in a small saucepan and heat, stirring, until the sugar has dissolved. Add the alcohol or vanilla and set aside to cool.

To make the cream, whip the mascarpone and caster sugar together to loosen. In a separate bowl, combine the double cream, icing sugar, vanilla and salt and whip until soft peaks form. Fold the cream into the mascarpone mixture in three batches and set aside.

To assemble your cake, put a layer of genoise on a cake plate. Using a pastry brush, drench it with one-third of the syrup. Add one-fifth of the cream and spread it over the cake. Arrange half the thinly sliced strawberries on top. Cover with the second sponge and repeat the process, using up all the sliced strawberries. Add the third sponge and soak with the last of the syrup. Spread half the remaining cream over the top, then spread the rest around the sides, smoothing it over with a palette knife to create a naked look.

To make the chocolate drip, melt the chocolate and double cream together in the microwave in 30-second bursts, stirring in between. Allow to cool slightly. Using a spoon, pour the chocolate drip over the edge of one half of the cake to create a dripping effect.

Cut the whole strawberries in half, leaving the calyx on. Arrange them in a crescent on top of the cake, above the chocolate drip, then decorate with the extra berries here and there. The cake can be stored in the fridge for up to 5 days.

Victoria sponge my way

 25 minutes 35 minutes  12 1

150g/5½oz/⅔ cup unsalted butter, at room temperature
150g/5½oz/¾ cup caster (superfine) sugar
1 tsp vanilla bean paste or vanilla extract
¼ tsp salt
3 large eggs
150g/5½oz/1 cup plus 2 tbsp self-raising flour *(gf)*
½ tsp baking powder *(gf)*

For the topping

300g/10½oz/1¼ cups double (heavy) cream
50g/1¾oz/6 tbsp icing (confectioners') sugar
1 tsp vanilla bean paste or vanilla extract
150g/5½oz/½ cup strawberry jam
200g/7oz fresh strawberries

+ tip

It is important to understand that whipped cream will keep thickening even after you stop whipping! So to avoid it looking curdled on your dessert, stop just after you reach soft peak stage and put it in your piping bag. If, however, you overwhip your cream, add a little more cream to it and fold in by hand to bring it back to a smooth texture.

So, you have been invited around for tea, coffee or even prosecco. You want to bring something but don't have all the ingredients for a fancy cake. Fear not, because this cake is for you!

It's a moist, light and simple Victoria sponge that has been beautifully decorated with fresh strawberries and Chantilly cream. It's great to make when strawberries are in season and at their cheapest, but also works with many other fruits: plums, cherries, raspberries, peaches and more. Just choose the jam that matches your fresh fruit; I sometimes make a pineapple version using pineapple jam and cubed fresh pineapple macerated in some vanilla and a tablespoon of sugar (and even a little bit of rum).

Preheat the oven to 200°C/180°C fan/400°F/Gas 6. Grease a 23cm/9in cake tin and line with baking parchment.

In a large bowl, cream together the butter, sugar, vanilla and salt until light and fluffy. Add the eggs one at a time, whisking well after each addition. With a spatula, fold in the flour and baking powder until fully incorporated. Pour the batter into the prepared tin and smooth the surface level. Bake for 30–35 minutes, or until the cake is risen, golden brown and a skewer inserted into the centre comes out clean. Leave to cool in the tin for 5 minutes, then transfer to a wire rack and leave to cool completely.

In a large bowl, use an electric whisk to whip the cream, icing sugar and vanilla together just until soft peaks form, then transfer it to a piping bag fitted with a St Honoré nozzle (see page 13) or a plain round nozzle.

To assemble your cake, place the sponge on a cake stand or a flat plate. Spread the jam over the top, leaving a rim of 2–3cm (1in) clear around the edge to make piping the cream easier. Pipe the cream around the edge of the cake, leaving enough space at the centre for the strawberries.

Cut the strawberries into quarters, leaving the green calyx on – this will add colour to your bake. Starting at the centre, arrange the strawberry quarters on the top of the cake in rings, alternating the direction the points of the strawberries face with each layer. Best enjoyed straight away, although the decorated cake can be stored in an airtight container in the fridge for up to 3 days.

Black Forest gateau

 1 hour 20 minutes  10 minutes 12 1

For the genoise

20g/⅔oz/2 tbsp cornflour/
   cornstarch
40g/1½oz/4¾ tbsp plain
   (all-purpose) flour (gf plus ⅛ tsp
   xanthan gum)
30g/1oz/scant ⅓ cup
   unsweetened cocoa powder
¼ tsp baking powder (gf)
   (optional)
a pinch of salt
3 large eggs
100g/3½oz/½ cup caster
   (superfine) sugar
30g/1oz/2 tbsp butter, melted,
   plus extra for greasing
1 tsp vanilla extract

For the syrup

50g/1¾oz/¼ cup caster (superfine)
   sugar
50g/1¾oz/3½ tbsp water
1 tbsp cherry conserve (from the
   jar below)
1 tbsp kirsch, vodka or any fruit
   brandy (optional)

To fill and decorate

600g/21oz/2½ cups double
   (heavy) cream
60g/2oz/½ cup icing
   (confectioners') sugar
1 tsp vanilla extract
1 jar (about 300g/10½oz) cherry
   conserve, stirred to loosen
100g/3½oz fresh cherries, or
   frozen cherries, defrosted
50g/1¾oz dark (bittersweet)
   chocolate, to decorate

Naked cakes aren't just beautiful and forgiving, they're also an economical way to use buttercream, because you need a lot less than for a fully coated cake. And what better way to use this style of cake decorating than a Black Forest gateau? It's super light, moist and has a strong kick of cherry flavour.

If you're making this cake for adults only, add some kirsch or other fruit brandy to your syrup, or simply leave it out so the whole family can have a slice. If your kids have a grown-up palate and like something other than vanilla cake, this would be a nice little birthday cake. I can also see it taking centre stage around Christmas.

The choice of a genoise sponge means that you don't need a lot of ingredients, and this cooks in just in 15 minutes, saving time and energy (see my tips for making genoise on page 18–19). Use fresh cherries if you are making this cake when they're in peak season and cheaper. If you are making it out of season, use thawed frozen cherries – they are a quarter of the price of fresh ones, add moisture to your sponge and are just as delicious.

To ensure success with your genoise, it's important that everything is prepared before you start whipping the eggs and sugar. Preheat the oven to 220°C/200°C fan/425°F/Gas 7. Grease a 32 x 23cm/13 x 9in rectangular cake tin and line with baking parchment.

Sift the flours, cocoa powder and baking powder (if using) into a medium bowl. Add the salt and set aside.

Put the eggs and sugar in a mixing bowl and whisk with an electric hand mixer for 10 minutes, or until the mixture triples in size and falls from the whisk in a smooth ribbon.

Sprinkle the flour mixture over the egg mixture in two stages, folding in each batch with three or four turns of a small balloon whisk (you can use a spatula, but the balloon whisk will help keep more air in the mixture). Add the melted butter and vanilla and fold them in gently.

Pour the batter into the prepared cake tin and bake for 8–10 minutes, or until a skewer inserted into the centre comes out clean. Unmould the sponge onto a wire rack and leave to cool completely.

While your cake is baking, prepare the syrup. Combine the sugar, water and cherry conserve in a small pan and bring to a boil. Add the alcohol, if using, then set aside to cool.

If you don't already have it, you can omit the cornflour and use additional flour in your genoise instead. For example, in this recipe you would use 60g/2oz/½ cup plain (all-purpose) flour.

Once your genoise is cold, make the filling by whipping the cream, icing sugar and vanilla together until soft peaks start to form when the whisk is lifted. Do not overwhisk as the cream continues to whip while you are piping and can develop a split appearance. Transfer one-third of the cream to a piping bag fitted with a star nozzle (if you don't have one, see how to improvise on page 13) and set aside.

To assemble the cake, cut your genoise, along the longest side, into three strips measuring just over 10cm/4in wide by 23cm/9in long. Place the first strip on a presentation plate. Drizzle over one-third of the syrup, then spread a couple of tablespoons of the cherry conserve over the cake. Add one-quarter of the remaining whipped cream on top and spread evenly. Add another layer of cake and repeat the process until you have added and topped all the layers.

Spread the remaining cream in the bowl around the side of the cake and smooth neatly with a palette knife. Using the piping bag you set aside, pipe a decorative border of cream around the top edge of the cake. Spoon the remaining cherry conserve into the centre, then fill the well with the cherries.

Make chocolate shavings by scraping the chocolate bar with a sharp knife or potato peeler and use them to decorate the sides of the cake, adding a few on top of the cherries, too. Chill for a few hours before serving.

Tiramisu gateau

 1½ hours + chilling   15 minutes | 12   2

For the genoise
40g/1½oz/⅓ cup cornflour
  (cornstarch)
80g/2¾oz/⅔ cup less 1 tbsp plain
  (all-purpose) flour (gf plus ¼ tsp
  xanthan gum)
½ tsp baking powder (gf)
  (optional)
a pinch of salt
4 large eggs
100g/3½oz/½ cup caster
  (superfine) sugar
1 tsp vanilla extract
cocoa powder, for dusting
200g/7oz dark (bittersweet)
  chocolate, finely chopped
  (optional – if making the collar)

For the coffee syrup
30g/1oz/2½ tbsp caster (superfine)
  sugar
50g/1¾oz/3½ tbsp hot water
1 tbsp instant coffee powder
50g/1¾oz/3½ tbsp marsala wine
  (optional)

For the cream
4 egg yolks
130g/4½oz/⅔ cup caster
  (superfine) sugar
400g/14oz/1¾ cups mascarpone
  cheese
300g/10½oz/1¼ cups double
  (heavy) cream
50g/1¾oz/6 tbsp icing
  (confectioners') sugar

I make tiramisu gateau at least once a month and cannot rate it highly enough. You could take the simpler approach with this recipe and simply layer it all up in a baking dish, or elevate it with piping and a chocolate collar for special occasions. Whichever you choose, it's best to leave it for a day in the fridge, or perhaps make it in the morning for dinner in the evening, so that the flavours have time to mingle.

I've made the chocolate collar with both parchment paper (the cheapest option) and acetate that I bought online. They both look beautiful in their own way; the parchment paper leaves interesting patterns in the collar while the acetate gives a clean, smooth finish. Tempering the chocolate will ensure your collar remains hard and snappy in the heat of a warm day. If you prefer, you can just melt all the chocolate without worrying about tempering, then simply wrap the collar around your cake and allow it to set in the fridge.

I bake the genoise sponge (see pages 18–19 for tips on this) in one 20cm/8in cake tin, but I recommend two because then they will cook quicker and there's no need to slice the cake horizontally before layering. And when serving this to kids, I omit the alcohol and use decaf coffee, too.

- -

Preheat your oven to 200°C/180°C fan/400°F/Gas 6. Grease and line two 20cm/8in round cake tins with baking parchment.

Sift the flours and baking powder (if using), into a mixing bowl. Add the salt and set aside.

Put the eggs and sugar in a mixing bowl and whisk with an electric hand mixer for 10 minutes, or until the mixture triples in size and falls from the whisk in a smooth ribbon.

Sprinkle the flour mixture over the egg mixture in two stages, folding in each batch with three or four turns of a small balloon whisk (you can use a spatula, but the balloon whisk will help keep more air in the mixture). Add the vanilla and fold in gently.

Divide the batter equally between the prepared tins. Bake for 10–15 minutes or until a skewer inserted into the centre comes out clean. Unmould the sponges onto a wire rack and allow to cool completely.

While your cake is baking, prepare the syrup by combining the sugar, hot water and coffee powder in a small pan and bringing to a boil. Add the marsala, if using, and set aside to cool.

To make the cream, put the egg yolks and sugar in a heatproof medium bowl and set it over a pan of steaming water. Whisk continuously for about 5 minutes or until the mixture is light and creamy and has doubled in size. Remove the bowl from the heat and set aside to cool. Once it has cooled completely, add the mascarpone and stir until combined – if you add the mascarpone while it's still hot, it will melt.

In a separate bowl, whip the double cream and icing sugar together until soft peaks form when the whisk is lifted from the bowl. Pour a third of the egg and mascarpone mixture onto the whipped cream and fold gently until incorporated. Repeat with the second and final third batch of the mixture. Fold in 1 tablespoon of your cold coffee syrup for flavour. You should have a thick cream that holds (if not, see tip, left).

To assemble your cake, place your first layer of cooled genoise on a flat plate or cake board. Using a pastry brush or spoon, drench it with half the coffee syrup. Add a few scoops of cream and spread out using a knife or spatula. Place the second sponge on top and soak it with the remaining syrup. Spread a fine layer of cream over the surface. Next take a couple of tablespoons of cream and smooth them over the sides of your cake with a palette knife to create a naked cake effect.

Put the remaining cream in a piping bag and cut a 2cm/¾in hole in the end – or you can use a large round piping nozzle if you have one. Pipe a ring of large blobs around the top edge of the cake, pulling the bag into the centre of the cake as you finish off the piping movement. Repeat to pipe another ring inside this one, and then repeat until you reach the centre of the cake and have a few rows of piping. At this point you can dust the cake with cocoa powder and serve as is.

Alternatively, make a chocolate collar by cutting a strip of parchment paper a few centimetres longer than the circumference of the cake tin and twice as tall as your gateau (roughly 70 x 10cm/28 x 4in). Fold the parchment in two lengthways for more support, so it measures about 70 x 5cm. You can also use a piece of acetate – in which case, cut it 70 x 5cm (28 x 2in).

Temper your dark chocolate following the method on page 18, then pour it along the parchment paper collar or acetate and spread it evenly using a knife. Wrap the chocolate collar around your cake, chocolate-side inwards, and, if tempered properly, the collar should set at room temperature. Alternatively, simply melt all the chocolate, spread it onto the parchment or acetate, wrap it around the cake and place in the fridge to set for about 30 minutes or until the chocolate has set hard.

Peel the parchment or acetate away gently and dust your finished gateau with some cocoa powder. It's best enjoyed the next day, or after a few hours in the fridge.

+ tip

If your cream is too runny, you have likely incorporated the mascarpone too early or under-whipped your double cream. But all is far from lost: simply layer your dessert in a baking tray, dust with cocoa powder and skip the piping and chocolate collar step.

Hazelnut praline bûche de Noël (Yule log)

 1 hour 15 minutes 8 2

For the meringue mushrooms (optional)

1 egg white

50g/1¾oz/¼ cup caster (superfine) sugar

a few drops of vinegar

a little red food colouring (use gel or powder colouring, not liquid)

For the genoise

20g/⅔oz/3 tbsp cornflour (cornstarch)

60g/2oz/7¼ tbsp plain (all-purpose) flour (*gf plus ¼ tsp xanthan gum*)

½ tsp baking powder (*gf*) (optional)

a pinch of salt

3 eggs

80g/2¾oz/6 tbsp sugar

1 tsp vanilla bean paste or extract

30g/1oz/2 tbsp butter, melted, plus extra for greasing

For the syrup

50g/1¾oz/¼ cup caster (superfine) sugar

50g/1¾oz/3½ tbsp water

For the hazelnut brittle

1 tbsp water

60g/2oz/5 tbsp caster (superfine) sugar

1 tsp vanilla bean paste or vanilla extract

a pinch of salt

120g/4¼oz/scant 1 cup peeled, toasted hazelnuts

10g/⅓oz/2 tsp butter

For the chocolate bark

150g/5½oz tempered dark chocolate (see page 18)

icing (confectioner's) sugar, for dusting (optional)

Ingredients continue overleaf...

For me, a yule log is an essential part of the traditional Christmas dinner. I've made a few in my time and one of the favourites is this praline yule log. I've used some of the egg white leftover from making the filling to produce woodland mushroom decorations.

- -

If you wish to decorate your log with meringue mushrooms, do this first; otherwise, skip this section. Preheat the oven to 120°C/100°C fan/250°F/gas ½ and line a baking sheet with baking parchment.

Put the egg whites and vinegar in a clean bowl and whisk together with an electric hand whisk until frothy. Add the sugar 1 tablespoon at a time, whisking continuously, until the meringue is thick and glossy and stiff peaks form when the whisk is lifted from the bowl.

Remove one third of your meringue to a separate bowl, add a little red food colouring, and mix until combined and you have a red meringue. Place the red meringue in one piping bag and the white meringue in another piping bag. Cut a 1cm/½ inch hole at the end of the white meringue piping bag and pipe eight tall meringue kisses onto the lined baking sheet – these will be your stalks.

Cut the tip off the white meringue piping bag to make it slightly larger – about 2cm/¾ inch this time. To make the mushroom caps, pipe four blobs, each 3–4cm/1¼–1½ inch in diameter onto the tray, swirling the tip to the side as you finish so you have a round top. Repeat with the red meringue piping bag to pipe four red mushroom caps. Now, use a cocktail stick (toothpick) to drop a few white meringue speckles on two of the red mushroom caps and add some red dots to two of the white mushroom caps.

Bake the meringues for 1 hour until crisp. Don't worry about baking for that long, as the lower the oven temperature, the less energy it consumes. Once cool, store in an airtight container until required.

For the log itself, preheat your oven to 200°C/180°C fan/400°F/Gas 6. Grease a 33 x 22cm/13 x 8½in rimmed baking tray and line it with baking parchment.

To make the genoise, sift the flours and baking powder (if using) into a mixing bowl. Add the salt and set aside.

Put the eggs and sugar in a separate mixing bowl and whisk with an electric hand mixer for 10 minutes, or until the mixture triples in size and falls from the whisk in a smooth ribbon.

Sprinkle the flour mixture over the egg mixture in two stages, folding in each batch with three or four turns of a small balloon whisk. Add the vanilla and the melted butter and fold gently until incorporated.

For the crème mousseline

300g/10½oz/1¼ cups milk

3 egg yolks

70g/2½oz/5 ⅔ tbsp sugar

20g/⅔oz/3 tbsp custard powder or cornflour

200g/7oz/¾ cup plus 2 tbsp butter, at room temperature

1 tsp vanilla bean paste or vanilla extract

a pinch of salt

+ tip

When the custard is ready, it should be thick, stiff and smooth, and clinging to the whisk, but still soft enough to spread.

+ thrifty

If you are left with some flakes of chocolate bark, keep them in an airtight container and use them in another bake that calls for melted chocolate.

Spread the batter into the prepared baking tray. Bake for 15 minutes or until a skewer inserted in the centre comes out clean. Once baked, lift the cake with the parchment onto a cooling rack. Cover with a clean kitchen towel and gently roll it into a log while still warm. This will keep the moisture in your sponge and pre-shape it so that you don't get any cracks when rolling later. Leave to cool completely.

Prepare the syrup by stirring the sugar and water together over a low heat until the sugar has dissolved, then set aside to cool.

To make the hazelnut brittle, put the water and sugar in a saucepan and cook over a medium-high heat until you have a light amber caramel (see page 20). Stir in the vanilla and salt, then add the hazelnuts and mix until coated. Mix in the butter, then spread the mixture onto a silicone mat or lined baking tray and allow to cool. Once cooled, break it up by putting it in a freezer bag and bashing with a rolling pin. Set aside ready for when you assemble the cake.

To make the chocolate bark, cut two 30cm x 20cm/12 x 8in sheets of baking parchment. If you have made the mushrooms, use a little of the chocolate to glue your mushroom caps and stalks together and leave to set. Spread the rest of the tempered chocolate onto the first parchment sheet evenly, leaving a gap around the edges for spread, then lay the second sheet on top and gently smooth it over. Starting from a short end, roll gently into a cylinder – make it as tight as you can without the chocolate being pushed out – and leave to set (in the fridge if your chocolate has not been tempered).

To make the crème mousseline, bring the milk to scalding point in a saucepan. Whisk the egg yolks and sugar together in a bowl. Add the custard powder, vanilla and salt and mix until smooth. Pour the hot milk over the egg mixture in a slow stream, mixing all the time. Return the mixture to the pan and stir continuously over the heat until the custard thickens and when you drag a spoon through the custard it will hold the line for a few seconds (see tip, left). Add 30g/1oz/2 tablespoons of the butter and mix well. Pour into a bowl, cover the surface with cling film and allow to cool at room temperature.

Meanwhile, whip your remaining butter until soft. When the custard is fully cool, whip it a little to loosen, then add the butter in small batches while whipping continuously. Add the vanilla and salt and keep whipping until your cream is light in colour and airy.

Gently unroll the sponge – it should still have a slight curve. Using a pastry brush, soak your sponge with the syrup. Spread two-thirds of the crème mousseline over the sponge, leaving a strip uncovered at the end to allow for a clean roll. Sprinkle with two-thirds of the hazelnut brittle, then roll the sponge into a log, placing the seam at the bottom. Spread the rest of the crème mousseline over the log, including the ends, and apply the remaining brittle to the two ends.

Unroll and peel the chocolate bark off the paper to give long curls. Press them onto the log to create a tree trunk effect. Dust with a little icing sugar to give that festive feel and add the mushrooms, if using. The yule log with keep in the fridge for up to a week.

Quick and Convenient

Blueberry mug cake

 5 minutes 2 minutes | 1 2

30g/1oz/2 tbsp butter
30g/1oz/2½ tbsp sugar
25g/1oz/1 tbsp plus 2 tsp whole
  milk
1 small egg
40g/1½oz/heaped ¼ cup self-
  raising flour (gf)
a pinch of ground cinnamon
½ tsp vanilla extract
10 blueberries
custard (store-bought or see
  recipe below) or ice cream,
  to serve

+ tip

Quick, small-batch custard:
If you want to make your
own quick custard, warm
80g/¾oz/⅓ cup milk in
the microwave for about
30 seconds.

In a small mug, whisk
together **1 egg yolk** and
1 teaspoon of sugar
until combined. Add **¼**
teaspoon vanilla extract
and **¼ teaspoon cornflour**
(cornstarch) and mix to a
paste. Pour over the warm
milk, whisking continuously.
(That will temper the egg and
prevent it from turning into an
omelette in the microwave.)

Cook the mixture in the
microwave for 2 minutes,
stirring halfway through.
When ready, pour the custard
over your mug cake and
enjoy warm.

Now microwave cakes! This mug cake is one of those winter-warming treats that takes minimal effort and makes you feel content. Cinnamon, berries and warm custard – what's not to like?

If you have any other berries, such as blackberries or leftover frozen mixed berries, from the chocolate and berry meringue roulade (see page 136), they could work very well here. Canned or fresh peaches left over from the peach crumble tarte Tropezienne recipe (see page 65) or apricots can also be substituted.

Make your own quick custard if you happen to have any egg yolk lying around from another recipe, or simply use shop-bought custard or instant custard powder. You'll find the recipe for my small batch of quick microwave custard in the tip below. Feel free to use a scoop of vanilla ice cream too.

- -

Put the butter in a large mug and microwave on medium–high power (600 watts) for 10–20 seconds.

Add the sugar and milk and stir to combine. Add the egg and mix vigorously with a whisk or small spatula to avoid streaks of egg white in your cake.

Stir in the flour, cinnamon and vanilla, mixing well to ensure there are no lumps.

Stir seven of the blueberries into the batter. Wipe clean the edges of your mug and place the remaining three blueberries on top of the batter.

Microwave your mug cake on medium–high (600 watts) for 1½ minutes. Keep an eye on your cake, as each microwave oven cooks differently. You want the batter to be only just cooked; when you lightly touch the top, it should feel slightly sticky. If it feels completely dry, you have over-cooked your cake.

Remove the mug cake from the microwave and pour over the custard and/or add a scoop of ice cream.

Hug in a mug sticky toffee cake

 8 minutes 6 minutes | 2 2

60g/2oz dates, finely chopped

¼ tsp bicarbonate of soda (baking soda)

30g/1oz/2 tbsp hot water

40g/1½oz/2½ tbsp butter

40g/1½oz/3¼ tbsp soft light brown sugar

1 medium egg

50g/1¾oz/heaped ⅓ cup self-raising flour (gf)

¼ tsp salt

1 tsp vanilla extract

2 scoops vanilla ice cream, to serve (optional)

For the microwave salted caramel sauce

15g/½oz/1 tbsp salted butter

30g/1oz/2 tbsp double (heavy) cream

60g/2oz/5 tbsp soft light brown sugar

¼ tsp vanilla extract

a pinch of salt

Okay – sticky toffee puddings are not the prettiest of cakes, but they are a hug in a mug! Especially on those early dark winter evenings when you just want to curl up on the couch watching TV with something warm and comforting in your hand – preferably something that does not take long to put together.

This recipe makes two, but feel free to halve it for one mug cake. If you do, you can keep the remaining beaten egg to use as egg wash, or in stir-fried rice or noodles for one.

You can top these with the salted caramel sauce, but I think they are delicious with a simple scoop of vanilla ice cream too.

To make the salted caramel sauce, melt the butter in a mug in the microwave. Add the cream and sugar, and stir until smooth. Cook on medium–high (600 watts) for 1 minute. Give it a stir, then return to the microwave for another minute, cooking until slightly thickened. Stir in the vanilla and salt and set aside to cool.

In a small bowl, combine the chopped dates, bicarbonate of soda and hot water and leave the dates to soften while you prepare the batter.

In another non-metallic bowl, melt the butter in the microwave, then stir in the sugar until combined. Add the egg and stir vigorously with a whisk or small spatula to avoid streaks of egg white in your cake. Add the flour, salt and vanilla, mixing well, then stir in the dates.

Divide the batter evenly between two mugs. Cook one cake at a time for 1½ minutes on medium–high (600 watts). Keep an eye on them, as each microwave oven cooks differently. You want the batter to be only just cooked; when you lightly touch the top, it should feel slightly sticky. If it feels completely dry, you have over-cooked your cake.

Top your sticky toffee cakes with a scoop of ice cream, if using, drizzle with the salted caramel sauce and enjoy whilst still warm.

Victoria sponge mug cake

 5 minutes  2 minutes 1 3

30g/1oz/2 tbsp salted butter
30g/1oz/2½ tbsp sugar
25g/1oz/1 tbsp plus 2 tsp whole
   milk
1 small egg
40g/1½ oz/heaped ¼ cup
   self-raising flour (gf)
1 tsp vanilla extract

For the topping

50g/1¾oz/3½ tbsp double
   (heavy) cream
½ tsp vanilla extract
1 tbsp strawberry jam
1 strawberry, to decorate
   (optional)

Sometimes simple will do just fine. A moist vanilla sponge topped with strawberry jam and whipped cream – what more could one possibly want? Feel free to use canned whipped cream here if you have it, in which case omit the vanilla.

- -

Put the butter in a large mug and microwave on medium–high power (600 watts) for 10–20 seconds.

Add the sugar and milk and stir to combine. Add the egg and mix vigorously with a whisk or small spatula to avoid streaks of egg white in your cake.

Stir in the flour and vanilla, mixing well to ensure there are no lumps.

Microwave on medium–high (600 watts) for 1½ minutes. Keep an eye on your cake, as each microwave oven cooks differently. You want the batter to be only just cooked; when you lightly touch the top, it should feel slightly sticky. If it feels completely dry, you have over-cooked your cake. Remove from the microwave and allow to cool.

In a small bowl, combine the cream and vanilla and whip until thickened (see page 19). Top the cake with a generous spoonful of strawberry jam, a dollop of whipped cream and a fresh strawberry, if you like. Enjoy.

Speculoos mug cake

 5 minutes  2 minutes | 1 | 3

30g/1oz/2 tbsp salted butter
1 tsp speculoos spread
40g/1½oz/3¼ tbsp sugar
25g/1oz/1 tbsp plus 2 tsp whole
    milk
1 small egg
40g/1½oz/heaped ¼ cup
    self-raising flour
1 tsp vanilla extract

For the topping
1 tbsp speculoos spread
1 scoop vanilla ice cream
1 speculoos or other biscuit, for
    crumbling

Microwave cakes will never replace an oven-baked cake, in my opinion, because good things take time to create. That said, when you don't have an oven, when you're not in your own kitchen with your own equipment, when you're limited by time, or even have just a few bits of ingredients here and there, microwave mug cakes make a great substitute. And they'll help you get rid of that sugar craving!

Everyone has some kind of spread in their store cupboard. In our house we love speculoos spread, made from those spiced shortcrust biscuits. All you have to do is stir a spoonful into the mug cake mixture and top the cake with some extra melted spread, plus a scoop of ice cream and a crumbled biscuit. Yum.

Put the butter and speculoos spread in a large mug and microwave on medium–high power (600 watts) for 10–20 seconds. Stir until smooth.

Add the sugar and milk and stir until combined. Then add the egg and mix vigorously with a whisk or small spatula to avoid streaks of egg white in your cake. Finally, add the flour and vanilla, mixing thoroughly to ensure there are no lumps.

Microwave on medium–high (600 watts) for 1½ minutes. Keep an eye on the cake as each microwave cooks differently. You want the batter to be only just cooked; when you lightly touch the top, it should feel slightly sticky. If it feels completely dry, you have over-cooked your cake. Remove from the microwave and allow to cool.

To serve, melt the 1 tablespoon of speculoos spread in the microwave for about 10 seconds. Top the cake with a scoop of vanilla ice cream, drizzle with the melted speculoos spread and sprinkle with the crumbled biscuit. Enjoy.

Peanut butter and jam mug cake

 5 minutes 2 minutes  1 1

40g/1½oz/2½ tbsp peanut butter
2 tbsp milk
30g/1oz/3½ tbsp plain (all-
    purpose) flour *(gf plus a pinch of
    xanthan gum)*
30g/1oz/2½ tbsp caster (superfine)
    sugar
½ tsp vanilla bean paste or vanilla
    extract
¼ tsp baking powder *(gf)*
a pinch of salt
2 squares chocolate, chopped
    (optional)
2 tbsp strawberry or raspberry
    jam
a dollop of whipped cream, to
    serve (optional)

Peanut butter is a staple in most kitchen cupboards and if you are a peanut butter lover, this cake will hit the right spot. Use any strawberry or raspberry jam you have available, but any leftover compote you have from the chocolate and berry meringue roulade (see page 136) could work very well here too. Roughly chop and throw in your last few squares of chocolate, if you have any, or even soft toffees cut in small pieces.

Put the peanut butter and milk in a large mug and microwave on medium–high power (600 watts) for 10–20 seconds. Stir well to combine.

Add the flour, sugar, vanilla, baking powder and salt and mix vigorously with a fork or small spatula to avoid any lumps in your cake. Add the chocolate (if using) then swirl in the jam.

Microwave your mug cake on medium–high (600 watts) for 1½ minutes. Keep an eye on your cake, as each microwave oven cooks differently. You want the batter to be only just cooked; when you lightly touch the top, it should feel slightly sticky. If it feels completely dry, you have over-cooked your cake.

Remove the mug cake from the oven and enjoy warm.

Lemon curd cheesecake

 20 minutes none 2 3

6 digestive biscuits (graham crackers) *(gf)*, plus 1 extra (optional) crumbled biscuit, to serve

30g/1oz/2 tbsp butter

80g/2¾oz/⅓ cup cream cheese

40g/1½oz/3¼ tbsp caster (superfine) sugar

½ tsp vanilla bean paste or vanilla extract

200g/7oz/scant 1 cup double (heavy) cream

4 tbsp lemon curd (shop-bought or see below)

2 lemon slices, to serve (optional)

For the curd (optional)

40g/1½oz/2½ tbsp butter

1 egg

70g/2½oz/⅓ cup caster (superfine) sugar

juice and finely grated zest of 1 large lemon

When you want a no-bake dessert that comes together in less than half an hour, this is the one. You could use shop-bought lemon curd, but I've got a quick microwave curd recipe here for you. Save the remainder for toast or to make another pot of this delicious pudding. If you have leftover mascarpone from the tiramisu cake, use that in place of the cream cheese.

If you're making the lemon curd, first melt the butter in a microwave-safe bowl in the microwave. In a separate bowl, whisk the egg and sugar together until combined, then whisk in the lemon juice and zest and the melted butter.

Microwave on a medium–high power (600 watts) for 3 minutes, stirring at 1-minute intervals. Pour the curd into a small jar and set aside to cool.

To make the cheesecake, finely crush the digestive biscuits in a small freezer bag.

Melt the butter in a microwaveable bowl, then add the biscuit crumbs and mix well. Divide the crumbs between two small ramekins and press the mixture down with a spoon to give firm bases. Place the ramekins in the freezer for a few minutes to set.

In a small bowl, beat together the cream cheese, sugar and vanilla until smooth.

In a separate bowl, use an electric hand mixer to whip the cream until stiff peaks form. Fold the whipped cream into the cream cheese mixture and spoon this evenly over your biscuit bases, smoothing the surfaces.

While the lemon curd is still warm and runny, pour half of it over each cheesecake. (If it has set, just heat it in the microwave for a few seconds.) Put your dessert in the fridge to set for at least 15–30 minutes. Once set, serve as they are or decorate your cheesecakes with a few extra biscuit crumbs and a slice of lemon, if you wish. Enjoy cold.

Peach cobbler

 10 minutes 20 minutes  1 1

½ x 400g/14oz can sliced peaches (130g/4½oz drained peaches)
1 tsp caster (superfine) sugar
¼ tsp vanilla bean paste or vanilla extract
¼ tsp cornflour (cornstarch)

For the topping
10g/⅓oz/1 rounded tbsp plain (all-purpose) flour *(gf)*
1 tsp porridge oats *(gf)*
10g/⅓oz/2 tsp salted butter, at room temperature
10g/⅓oz/2½ tsp light brown sugar
¼ tsp vanilla bean paste or vanilla extract

If you made the peach crumble tarte Tropézienne (see page 65) and still have half a can of peaches, here is a cobbler for one, perfect for using up the leftovers.

You can make this in the oven, but it feels such a waste of power when you could just use an air fryer. While I won't be baking a three-tier wedding cake in one, air fryers are a great way to save energy costs: the bake goes straight in and out in 20 minutes, and you won't need to spend time and energy preheating your air fryer.

No peaches? Use any other fruit you have available. Frozen and canned fruits are great for cobblers (think berries or rhubarb), but so are fresh fruits when in season. This is a great recipe for the last sorry specimens in the fruit bowl, such as pears, apples, nectarines and apricots.

- -

Drain the peaches and put them in a heatproof ramekin or mug. Add the sugar, vanilla and cornflour and mix until combined.

To make the topping, combine the flour, oats, butter, sugar and vanilla in a bowl and mix until you have something resembling cookie dough. Drop clumps of the dough over the peach mixture, covering the fruit.

Bake in the air fryer at 180°C/350°F for 20 minutes, or until the crumble is light golden and the peaches are warmed. If you don't have an air fryer, you can also cook these in an oven preheated to the same temperature for the same amount of time.

+ thrifty
If you are using the oven, scale up the recipe and make several cobblers to make the most of the spent energy.

Raspberry and chocolate bread and butter mug pudding

 10 minutes 20 minutes  2 2

2 small croissants (about 50g/1¾oz each), or about 100g/3½oz buttered white bread, brioche or buns (gf)

1 large egg

120g/4¼oz/½ cup whole milk

30g/1oz/2 tbsp double (heavy) cream

40g/1½oz/3¼ tbsp caster (superfine) sugar

½ tsp vanilla bean paste or vanilla extract

⅛ tsp ground nutmeg

a pinch of salt

8 raspberries

4 squares chocolate, cut into small chunks

Bread and butter pudding is a classic dessert that really encapsulates the thrifty concept. You can cook this recipe in the microwave or air fryer. Air fryers cook from the get-go, so you don't need to spend energy preheating as you do with a conventional oven. I won't be making a showstopper in one, but they do have a place when it comes to small, quick desserts like this.

I make bread and butter pudding using whatever is available and encourage you to do the same. Instead of stale croissants, you could use pain au chocolat, plain white bread, brioche, buns, or a fruited bread like hot cross buns. Most yeasted breads will work. You won't need butter if using pastries, but for any other bread, don't forget to generously butter it prior to adding the custard.

You could use only milk, or only cream, or a combination of both for the custard, so long as the overall quantity of liquid remains the same. Top it with any fruit you like – canned, fresh or frozen. I've added a few chunks of chocolate here, but you could use dried fruit or nuts, or add extra spices to give your pudding a wintery feel.

- -

Cut the croissants (or other bread) into 2.5cm/1in pieces.

In a bowl, whisk together the egg, milk, cream, sugar, vanilla, nutmeg and salt until well combined. Add the croissant pieces and toss gently. Tear in the raspberries and add the chocolate chunks. Mix well, then divide the mixture between two small ramekins.

If you are going to use the microwave oven, cook each ramekin for 1–1½ minutes, or until the custard appears cooked.

Alternatively, put your ramekins in the air fryer and bake at 180°C/350°F for 20 minutes. If you don't have an air fryer, you can also cook these in an oven preheated to the same temperature for the same amount of time. Enjoy warm.

+ thrifty

If you are using the oven, scale up the recipe and make several puddings to make the most of the spent energy.

Cookies and cream chocolate custard parfait

 30 minutes   none    2 3

For the chocolate custard
5g/⅛oz/1 tsp custard powder
100g/3½oz/scant ½ cup whole milk
20g/⅔oz dark (bittersweet) chocolate, chopped
15g/½oz/4 tsp caster (superfine) sugar
⅛ tsp instant coffee powder

For the frosting
50g/1¾oz/3½ tbsp cream cheese
30g/1oz/3½ tbsp icing (confectioners') sugar
150g/5½oz/scant ⅔ cup double (heavy) cream
½ tsp vanilla bean paste or vanilla extract

For the base
6 cookies and cream biscuits (such as Oreos) *(gf)*, plus 2 extra (optional) biscuits to decorate
10g/⅓oz/2 tsp butter, melted

This is a decadent no-bake dessert you can put together in just 30 minutes. We have layers of crunchy chocolate biscuits, and a velvety-smooth chocolate custard, all topped with cream cheese frosting.

This is really a quick 'when you need it' sort of dessert, so a pack of cookies from the shop is totally fine and will only set you back a few pence at the discount store or when buying a supermarket's own brand.

- -

Put the custard powder in a bowl, add 1 tablespoon of the milk and whisk until smooth. Add the remaining milk, chocolate, sugar and coffee and mix well.

Cook in the microwave on medium-high for 1 minute. Whisk thoroughly, then return the bowl to the microwave for a further 20 seconds. Mix well, cover the surface of the custard with cling film (plastic wrap) and place in the fridge to cool.

To make the frosting, combine the cream cheese, 20g/⅔oz/2¼ tablespoons of the icing sugar, 50g/1¾oz/3½ tablespoons of cream and ¼ teaspoon of vanilla in a small bowl. Whisk until smooth, then set aside.

In a separate bowl, whip the remaining double cream with the rest of the icing sugar and vanilla until stiff peaks form. Set aside.

Make the base by putting the biscuits in a freezer bag and crushing them with a rolling pin until they look like fine sand. Set 1 teaspoon aside to use for decoration. Add the melted butter to the remaining crushed biscuits and mix well.

To assemble, find yourself two medium jars or beakers of approximately 240ml/8½fl oz/1 cup volume. Divide the biscuit crumbs between them and pat down firmly.

Take the chocolate custard out of the fridge and whip it briefly to loosen it. Spoon it into the jars, dividing it equally between them, then top each jar with half the cream cheese mixture.

Spoon or pipe the sweetened whipped cream on top. Decorate with the reserved crushed biscuits and finish with an extra biscuit if you wish. Enjoy immediately or place in the fridge for later.

Chocolate hazelnut mug cake

 15 minutes  1 minute | 2 2

60g/2oz/4 tbsp chocolate
hazelnut spread (plus optional
2 tbsp for serving)

30g/1oz/2 tbsp warm milk

1 large egg white

50g/1¾oz/¼ cup caster (superfine)
sugar

40g/1½oz/4¾ tbsp plain
(all-purpose) flour (gf plus a
pinch of xanthan gum)

¼ tsp baking powder (gf)

½ tsp vanilla bean paste or vanilla
extract

custard, to serve (optional)

chocolates and/or fresh berries,
to decorate (optional)

For the frosting (optional)

50g/1¾oz/3½ tbsp double (heavy)
cream

70g/2½oz/⅓ cup cream cheese

30g/1oz/2½ tbsp caster (superfine)
sugar

20g/⅔oz/1½ tbsp chocolate
hazelnut spread

½ tsp vanilla bean paste or vanilla
extract

Here's a light, moist and fluffy mug cake that you can take to the next level if you want. Your secret will be safe with the microwave – no one will ever know if you don't tell!

Enjoy this on its own, with an extra spoonful of chocolate hazelnut spread on top, or unmould and decorate it. If you want to add the cream cheese frosting, you'll need to let it cool. Or, if you prefer, serve straight away with warm custard. I had some spare cream, so I decided to make the chocolate frosting, and add a few chocolates left over from the festive season.

- -

In a small bowl, mix the chocolate hazelnut spread and warm milk together. Stir in the egg white and sugar, mixing until combined. Add the flour, baking powder and vanilla and mix until the batter is smooth.

Divide the batter between two mugs and microwave for 1 minute on high power. Keep an eye on the cakes, as each microwave cooks differently. You want the batter to be only just cooked; when you lightly touch the top, it should feel slightly sticky. Take care not to overcook the cakes, as they will become difficult to unmould from the mugs.

At this point you can serve the cakes warm with a tablespoon of chocolate hazelnut spread on each, or with some custard. Or go the distance; allow them to cool and top with cream cheese frosting.

To make the frosting, put all the ingredients in a bowl and whip until stiff peaks form. Spread or pipe the frosting over the cooled cakes – you can keep them in the mugs or unmould them. Decorate with chocolates and/or berries before serving.

Index

Quarto

This edition first published in 2023 by White Lion Publishing
an imprint of The Quarto Group.
One Triptych Place, London, SE1 9SH
United Kingdom
T (0)20 7700 6700
www.Quarto.com

ISBN 978-0-7112-8748-8
EBOOK ISBN 978-0-7112-8882-9

10 9 8 7 6 5 4 3 2 1

Art director, prop stylist and project manager Rebecca Woods
Designer Georgie Hewitt
Editor Charlotte Frost
Food styling assistant Christina Cullen
Food stylist Katie Marshall
Photographer's assistant and retoucher Sam Reeves
Publisher Jessica Axe

Printed in China